Impact

Other titles from Bloomsbury Education

What Every Teacher Needs to Know: How to embed evidence-informed teaching and learning in your school by Jade Pearce

Fast Feedback: How one primary school abolished written marking by Lesley Hill with Gemma Whitby

The Wellbeing Toolkit: Sustaining, supporting and enabling school staff by Andrew Cowley

What Works?: Research and evidence for successful teaching by Lee Elliot Major and Steve Higgins

Teaching Rebooted: Using the science of learning to transform classroom practice by Jon Tait

The Headteacher's Handbook: The essential guide to leading a primary school by Rae Snape

The Inclusive Classroom: A new approach to differentiation by Daniel Sobel and Sara Alston

Impact

A five-part framework for making a difference in schools

Nick Hart

BLOOMSBURY EDUCATION

LONDON OXFORD NEW YORK NEW DELHI SYDNEY

BLOOMSBURY EDUCATION
Bloomsbury Publishing Plc
50 Bedford Square, London, WC1B 3DP, UK
29 Earlsfort Terrace, Dublin 2, Ireland

BLOOMSBURY, BLOOMSBURY EDUCATION and the Diana logo are
trademarks of Bloomsbury Publishing Plc

First published in Great Britain, 2022 by Bloomsbury Publishing Plc

This edition published in Great Britain, 2022 by Bloomsbury Publishing Plc

A catalogue record for this book is available from the British Library

ISBN: PB: 978-1-8019-9014-1; ePDF: 978-1-8019-9012-7;
ePub: 978-1-8019-9015-8

2 4 6 8 10 9 7 5 3 1 (paperback)

Typeset by Newgen KnowledgeWorks Pvt. Ltd., Chennai, India
Printed and bound in the UK by CPI Group Ltd, CR0 4YY

To find out more about our authors and books visit www.bloomsbury.com
and sign up for our newsletters

Contents

Introduction:
An overview of the impact
domains

The chances are that if you are reading this, we share something in common: a drive to make a difference.

A difference to the children in our year group or phase.

A difference to the children in our school or community.

Maybe even a difference to children across the country and beyond.

We have committed to education because we want to make an impact. We want to influence what children learn, motivate them to do their best and inspire them to make a difference.

Middle leaders are involved in multiple interactions each day as they support, advise and challenge colleagues in their role of leading a subject or leading a team. Each of our colleagues' unique histories and circumstances make our interactions far more complex than the simple cause-and-effect relationships that we like to think exist when it comes to impact: *If I just get colleagues to follow the behaviour policy/use concrete manipulatives/model the writing process/scaffold difficult tasks, children will be much better off.* Each interaction with colleagues results in unknowable consequences, both desired and undesired, as we seek to bring about improvement.

Senior leaders make scores of decisions every day that directly affect the working practices of every colleague and indirectly influence outcomes for children. But this is not simple cause and effect either: *If I just organise the school in the right way and get everyone working together on the right priorities, we'll have a great school.* Each decision that leaders make has innumerable consequences, good and bad, intended and unintended, predictable and unpredictable.

The school environment in all its glorious complexity is the reason for the 'no two days are the same' cliché but is also a difficult pill to swallow when we figure out that simple cause and effect just isn't realistic. Complexity in our phase or in our school cannot be simplified. It can, however, be somewhat mitigated by bringing stability, structure and organisation (Evans, 2020). Faced with such complexity, it would also be beneficial to bring more structure to our own thinking and behaviours, which is the central premise of the framework described in this book.

Whether you are a middle leader tasked with raising standards in your phase or a senior leader working on school improvement, you can make a difference in the five impact domains that form this framework. Paying attention to these domains and understanding the ways in which they influence each other can help you to make a difference.

Each impact domain is explored in the chapters in Section 1, which are as follows:

Climate: Leaders can make a difference to how it feels for colleagues to be part of a team and to work in their school.

Systems and processes: Leaders can make a difference to the culture of the school – how it runs in terms of professional development, the curriculum, pedagogy, assessment and managing behaviour at scale.

Colleagues' knowledge: Leaders can make a difference to what colleagues know and understand, including formal and hidden knowledge.

Colleagues' behaviours: Leaders can make a difference to how individual colleagues behave, including pedagogical behaviours and those related to interactions with fellow colleagues.

Outcomes for children: Leaders can make a difference to children across multiple classrooms, including (but not limited to) their academic and social development.

The impact framework: Structure of chapters

A mental model is the knowledge that one has and how it is organised to enable action. The impact framework is designed to bring order to leaders' thinking for the purpose of supporting the building of knowledge and improved decision-making. Each chapter is organised into the following structure:

- Why the impact domain matters
- The components of the domain
- Should the domain be evaluated?
- Building knowledge of the domain
- What could we do with the knowledge that we've built in this domain?
- Example scenarios
- Chapter summary

Why the impact domain matters

An explanation of the reasons why it is worth leaders paying attention to the impact domain.

The components of the domain

A description of the different concepts and behaviours that make up the domain.

Should the domain be evaluated?

A consideration of the reasons for and against evaluating impact in the domain. These sections reinforce a recurring argument for building knowledge of the domain in order to gain an accurate picture in the spirit of inquiry, rather than evaluating to reach a judgement.

Building knowledge of the domain

Suggestions for how leaders can build their knowledge of the reality of school life within the domain related to a specific problem, including the use of measurement where it is appropriate. An important theme in this section is the difficulty in inquiring into the entire domain. School life is too vast and complex to inquire into a domain as a whole, so each chapter looks at building knowledge of a specific problem.

What could we do with the knowledge that we've built in this domain?

A description of the options that leaders have when looking to apply the knowledge gained to make a positive impact.

Example scenarios

A thread of examples for leaders that are built upon chapter by chapter.

For aspiring and established middle leaders, we will get to know **Tim**, a lower Key Stage 2 phase leader in a two-form-entry primary school. Tim has a particular problem to solve regarding improving fluency of calculation for the least advantaged children in Year 3 and Year 4.

For aspiring and established senior leaders, we will get to know **Madiha**, the headteacher of a large primary school. Madiha has a particular problem to solve regarding improving reading attainment in Key Stage 2, where children's phonological awareness is not an issue.

Through each chapter, we will follow Tim and Madiha's pursuit of impact as they tackle their problems one domain at a time.

Chapter summary

The impact framework is a tool to support leaders to make a difference in their schools. By using each chapter, readers can develop their knowledge of each domain, plan to inquire further into how each domain manifests in their school and ultimately resolve the school improvement challenges that need addressing.

Examples and templates

The final chapter provides examples of the impact that leaders might seek when addressing a range of common, specific problems. Editable templates are also available to download from the dedicate page for the book on the Bloomsbury Education website: bloomsbury.pub/impact. Each template is populated with prompts that leaders can adapt or delete according to their school's individual requirements.

SECTION 1

The five-part framework

1 Climate

*Human beings have an innate inner drive to be autonomous,
self-determined, and connected to one another. And when that
drive is liberated, people achieve more and live richer lives.*

Daniel Pink (2009, p. 72)

Why climate matters

Climate is how colleagues feel about working in their team or their
school. While teachers have a more direct influence on outcomes
for children, leaders striving for influence across multiple classrooms
can only have an indirect impact. We should therefore seek to make
a difference to working conditions so that colleagues can be as
effective as possible. In order to improve outcomes for children, our
colleagues need to flourish.

The components of climate

Broadly, a positive climate is one where colleagues feel motivated,
where they feel safe and where they feel connected. Motivation is a
product of autonomy, mastery and purpose (Pink, 2009). This can be
broken down into six specific factors that make up the climate of a
school, as shown in Figure 1.1 and discussed in more detail below.

The importance of autonomy

The autonomy that colleagues have over how they spend their
time influences their motivation. There is a subtle difference here
between actual and perceived autonomy, and when it comes to

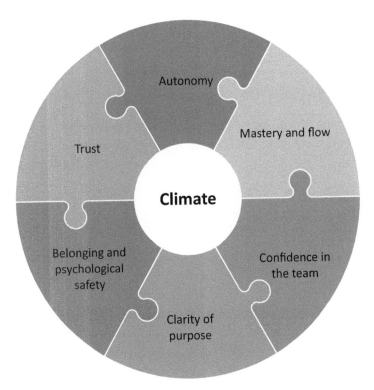

Figure 1.1 *The components of school climate.*

climate, it is perceived autonomy that matters. The nuance is that colleagues might spend hours on teaching and related tasks, but feel that it is worth it if the conditions are right. NfER research into teacher autonomy found that perceived autonomy is strongly associated with improved job satisfaction and a greater intention to stay in teaching (Worth and Van den Brande, 2020). The question is, what do we need to feel autonomy over? Four elements of autonomy to consider are task, time, technique and team (Figure 1.2).

Task

Task refers to the main responsibilities that we have in our role and what we do each day. These responsibilities are fixed in terms of

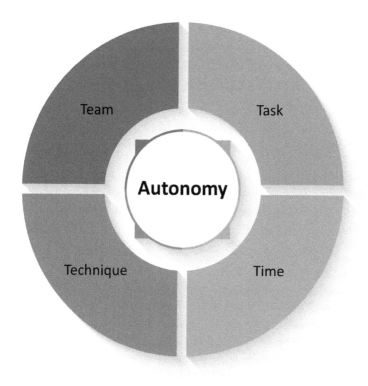

Figure 1.2 *Four elements of autonomy.*

the planning and teaching of lessons, but there are elements over which leaders might consider giving autonomy. Curriculum content is one such example. Giving colleagues choice over what they teach might be good in terms of their perception of autonomy, but it risks compromising a well-sequenced curriculum over year groups and key stages. The middle ground might be for leaders to involve colleagues in curriculum design at strategic level if they have an interest or expertise. Another area over which to consider giving colleagues autonomy (and the one most associated with higher job satisfaction) is their professional development goals. The challenge for leaders is to balance the autonomy of choice with the school's strategic priorities. Because of whole-school priorities, professional development sessions might often involve all colleagues together hearing about the areas to which leaders want them to pay attention. But in that one room there may be early career teachers, vastly experienced teachers and those who have experience somewhere in between. Pitching content that challenges different levels of expertise can be difficult.

Time

Time refers to when colleagues come and go from work and how their time is allocated each day. While it is obvious that colleagues need to be in school before children and ready for the day, it is perhaps a mistake to stipulate a start and finish time. Some people are more productive early in the morning while others are more effective later in the evening. Some have family commitments as well as work, and so affording flexibility about when tasks should be done is an important contributor to climate. Then there is the matter of colleagues' timetables. While there are, of course, constraints such as sharing specialist rooms or teachers, leaders can allow some informed choice about when subjects are taught and for how long. For example, it might be that colleagues choose to teach maths either side of breaktime or an assembly, to enable them to check understanding of some shared examples. Or it might be that children are enjoying writing and doing very well, in which case a colleague may wish to continue with the lesson rather than switch to another subject simply because the timetable dictates it.

Technique

Technique refers to how colleagues perform their main responsibilities, which in schools relates to pedagogy. Affording teachers the flexibility to choose teaching strategies to meet the needs of their pupils can be good for both the children and for our colleagues' perception of autonomy. The tension between teacher autonomy and guidance from leaders can be alleviated by leaders specifying the active ingredients of the school's teaching strategy – the principles and actions that make the chosen strategy most likely to be effective. An example of this is feedback. Restrictive marking and feedback policies increase workload, and may not necessarily improve children's learning. It would be more effective for leaders to clarify the active ingredients of a feedback policy, rather than to specify exact practices. For example:

- different approaches for different ages
- subject-specific approaches
- more work for the child than the teacher
- useful for the child and manageable for the teacher.

Team

Team refers to the extent to which colleagues can choose with whom they collaborate. Although year group, phase or key stage teams might be fixed, leaders can still facilitate choice with regard to whom colleagues work with and learn from informally. By creating opportunities for colleagues to get to know one another, they themselves can decide whom they would like to collaborate with on mutually interesting projects.

No more non-negotiables

In order to positively impact climate, it should not be the aim of leaders to try to control their colleagues' every move. Colleagues' perception of workload can be improved if they have control over how they spend their time and carry out their work, particularly regarding their professional development goals. It is often the case that leaders implement restrictive policies around marking, planning, classroom layout and even display board colour choices, and although all of these things might give the appearance of consistency, leaders need to consider the implications. The quality of teaching affects outcomes for children, but does controlling colleagues' working practices make them better able to meet children's needs? Although it is unlikely that it does, this doesn't mean that leaders can simply let colleagues do whatever they want. Training is key; with effective training, leaders will not have to rely on restrictive policies and, in turn, could improve the climate.

Mastery and flow

Pink (2009) describes mastery as the desire to get better and better at something that matters. He references Csikszentmihalyi's work on flow, a state where people have clear goals and where the challenge is neither too easy nor too difficult and, as a result, they find it deeply satisfying. A state of flow cannot exist without autonomy. While mastery is the result of years of effort, flow is the feeling in the moment and, as such, is a prerequisite for mastery. Leaders should therefore seek to create the conditions that enable colleagues to experience flow, by ensuring clear goals and responsibilities that are neither too easy nor too difficult, and by providing effective feedback, all of which will prime colleagues to experience this state. Colleagues who experience flow are more likely to enjoy their work and become more effective, therefore exerting a greater influence over outcomes for the children that they teach.

Confidence in the team

It is not just individual mastery and flow that matter. Leithwood, Sun and Pollock (2017) described an emotions path for leadership influence over student achievement that includes the feelings and dispositions of staff being akin to climate. This path encompassed collective teacher efficacy: the confidence that the group exudes in its capacity to organise and execute the tasks required to reach its desired goals. This can apply to a whole-school team or a sub team within a school, and it is absolutely conceivable that some sub teams might have confidence in their respective team's expertise and some might not. For example, a well-established team of Reception teachers might have confidence in their team to meet children's needs but, further down the corridor, a new team of less experienced Year 1 teachers might not feel the same about their own team.

Clarity of purpose

A fulfilled team is one that shares a common purpose. All the work that leaders do to communicate priorities and why they have chosen them can make a difference to the team's sense of purpose. Leithwood, Harris and Hopkins' (2019) first domain of practice in their description of what successful leaders do is set directions, and this includes building a shared vision, identifying specific, short-term goals, creating high-performance expectations and communicating those aspects of purpose in a way that all can understand. More specifically, though, it should include providing clarity on the specific problems that need our attention and the active ingredients of the strategies that we choose to tackle them. A model to support leaders to think this through in relation to school improvement can be seen in Figure 1.3.

School improvement model	
Aim	For what purpose does this school exist?
Values	What behaviours make us unique?
Vision	What is the future ideal for how the school runs?
Strategic priorities	What specific problems require our attention to realise our vision?
Drivers	What systems will help to address strategic priorities?
Strategies and their active ingredients	What strategies are required and what are the key concepts and behaviours that need to be implemented for them to be successful?

Figure 1.3 *A model for school improvement that supports leaders to define purpose.*

Climate

Belonging and psychological safety

The extent to which colleagues feel that they belong to the team and the school community can have an influence on their motivation and commitment, which makes a difference to school climate. How the team feels may seem disconnected to achieving the desired outcomes for children, but an appropriate climate is a prerequisite for those outcomes and is something that leaders can influence. Colleagues who are anxious or reluctant to admit faults or weaknesses cannot be at their best when supporting children, and therefore psychological safety is the foundation for making a difference. Psychological safety is achieved by the prevalence of belonging cues – signals to colleagues that they are professionally safe, that their opinions matter and that they play an important role in the school. Leaders can achieve psychological safety by seeking the opinions of colleagues and encouraging mixing between colleagues in order that they might make connections with one another, all in relation to the specific problems that are being tackled.

No improvement without trust

Viviane Robinson (2017) champions three leadership competencies required for school improvement: 1) Using relevant knowledge from research and experience, to 2) solve educational problems, while 3) building trust with those involved. As Robinson's model for expert leadership demonstrates, trust is important, but here's the conundrum:

> *Leadership is not just about building trust. Nor is it only about getting the work done. It is about doing both of those things simultaneously...*
> Viviane Robinson (2017, p. 4)

Bryk and Schneider (2003) demonstrated a causal relationship between the degree of trust among members of a school community and the degree of improvement in student outcomes.

However, trust does not directly affect student learning. Rather, trust fosters a set of conditions that make it easier for leaders to begin and sustain the kinds of activities necessary to bring about improvements. For example, it requires colleagues to be vulnerable, which they will only feel comfortable about if they believe that those with whom they work are competent, reliable and open, and genuinely care. While not all schools with high levels of trust improve, schools with little or no relational trust have practically no chance of improving.

Should climate be evaluated?

Leaders who know how the team feels about a particular issue are in a stronger position to improve working conditions. Leaders can give components of climate high status by inquiring into how colleagues feel about them and by paying attention to those components. However, the climate domain is so vast that it would be almost impossible to evaluate climate in its entirety. Furthermore, climate is likely to be affected by different circumstances such as the time of year and related workload patterns. This means that the likelihood of making accurate judgements about the climate is unreliable. Instead, it would be more effective for leaders to build their knowledge of climate in relation to a specific problem that they are seeking to tackle.

Then there is the issue of validity when evaluating. Leaders often have an incomplete picture of climate because of their position in the school hierarchy. They are less likely to be aware of issues with climate because colleagues may choose not to reveal their true feelings, particularly if there is a lack of psychological safety or trust. A possible solution is not to make judgements through evaluation but simply to aim to build knowledge around a problem as accurately as possible. Free from the implications of making judgements, leaders are more likely to gather an accurate picture of the reality.

Building knowledge of the climate

The elements of climate described earlier in this chapter could all be the subject of inquiry. These elements are the experiences of individuals, and so it is colleagues' perception of them that needs to be explored. Schein (1985) points out that when aiming to find out about culture, it is group perceptions that need to be sought, because culture is the shared beliefs, assumptions and behaviours that the group holds.

If leaders wanted to inquire into climate, group discussion is the most appropriate format, but this is time-consuming and therefore not necessarily a practical option. An alternative is the use of surveys, where teams discuss and self-report their feelings of autonomy, belonging or mastery, etc., relating to a specific problem that requires tackling. However, there are some important considerations for leaders when thinking about question design. In the following, we will consider the question: *To what extent do you feel that you have autonomy over teaching writing?*

Question design

How questions are phrased can significantly influence the responses received. The example question, *To what extent do you feel that you have autonomy over teaching writing?*, might be very hard to answer because, as described earlier in this chapter, there are different elements to autonomy. Naturally, colleagues will have different levels of autonomy over different aspects of their working conditions and, as such, leaders need to focus on which aspect(s) of autonomy they really want to know about. With this in mind, the question would be far more useful if it inquired into the perception of autonomy in a specific area, such as: *To what extent do you feel that you have autonomy over your professional development goals in the teaching of writing?*

Scaling

To generate trend data, surveys often use scaling, and the choice of scale is important. Take the question: *To what extent do you feel that you have autonomy over your professional development goals in the teaching of writing?* The scale could have three parts to it:

- none
- some
- full.

In this case, because the first and last options are absolute, they are unlikely to be how most colleagues would perceive their autonomy, and leaders would be likely to get most responses in the middle option, 'some'. Full autonomy over professional development in writing might not even be possible, as leaders will need to guide what teachers work on to align with school priorities. Instead, the options could be rephrased to:

- very little
- some
- lots.

Even with this adjustment, there is still a risk that the majority of colleagues would choose the middle option, which still might not result in any useful information. An odd number of options will inevitably have a middle, neutral choice; therefore, it may be that four options would be better in order to uncover the nuance in perceptions:

- very little
- some
- lots
- full.

Asking colleagues to quantify autonomy is still a tricky concept, though, and it might be more useful to switch from this to an agreement scale based on a statement, such as: *I have autonomy over my professional development goals in the teaching of writing:*

- strongly agree
- agree
- disagree
- strongly disagree.

Phrasing a survey in this way has the advantage of keeping it perception-focused rather than trying to quantify something that probably isn't quantifiable. It also gives leaders a chance to make statements about what they feel is important. *'I have autonomy over my professional development goals in the teaching of writing'* sounds far more purposeful than *'To what extent do you have autonomy over your professional development goals in writing?'*

Timing

The timing of a survey needs careful consideration in order for it to yield the most reliable results. Schools go through cycles of intense and less intense activity, sometimes with parts of a term or academic year packed with more seasonal workload such as assessments, reports or extra-curricular commitments. Survey responses cannot be evaluated in isolation – contextual information about conditions at the time of completion need to be taken into account. This reinforces the idea that attempting to inquire into the entire domain should be avoided, and that the focus instead should be on the knowledge-building phases of tackling a specific problem.

What could we do with the knowledge that we've built about the climate?

The information gathered through inquiry needs to be acted on; otherwise, the time taken to build that knowledge and for leaders to analyse what they have found would be wasted. There are two paths for leaders. One is further exploration of any trends that emerge and the other is to take action to improve working conditions and how those conditions are perceived.

Further exploration of trends is for the sole purpose of understanding the situation better. Using the example of autonomy, consider the result that the majority of colleagues disagreed that they had autonomy over their professional development goals in the teaching of writing. Leaders would need to know more about this, and talking to a sample of colleagues around the topic might yield more useful information upon which to act. Possible questions might include:

- What are your professional development goals in the teaching of writing?

- What do we spend time on in training that does not align with your goals?

- Is the amount of time that we spend on professional development of school priorities too much, too little or just right?

- Does our appraisal system help or hinder your pursuit of your professional development goals?

This is exactly the reason why discussion is more valuable than surveying, as it seems likely that further exploration might be required into any survey question – alone, it just cannot yield data that is sufficiently useful. With better contextual information, leaders are in a stronger position to make adaptations to working conditions that could improve the components of climate and, in turn, successfully tackle the problem that they are seeking to solve. This is a prudent course of action to take because of the positive effects of climate on job satisfaction, retention and, ultimately, outcomes for children.

Background

Remember **Tim**, a lower Key Stage 2 phase leader in a two-form-entry primary school? He has a particular problem to solve around improving fluency of calculation for disadvantaged children in Year 3 and Year 4.

Building knowledge of climate

Tim wants to build his knowledge of the role that climate plays in the problem of disadvantaged children's lack of fluency when calculating, and prepares some discussion questions for the next team meeting:

Autonomy

- Tell me about the autonomy you have over how you teach calculations and support disadvantaged children to learn them.
- Tell me about the autonomy you have over when you teach maths and how long lessons are.
- Tell me about the autonomy you have over how you assess and feed back to disadvantaged children in maths.
- Tell me about the autonomy you have over professional development regarding supporting disadvantaged children with fluency in calculation.

Mastery and flow

- Do you get enough developmental feedback regarding supporting disadvantaged children in maths? What kind of feedback works best for you?

- What aspects of supporting disadvantaged children in maths do you feel good at? Are there any aspects that you do not feel good at?

Purpose

- What makes great maths teaching?
- Are there any 'best ways' of teaching calculation?
- Is there anything additional to this that the disadvantaged children in your class need?

Psychological safety

- To what extent have leaders been clear about what is expected of you in supporting disadvantaged children with fluent calculation?
- What training do you need in calculation to support disadvantaged children more effectively?
- What do you need that you don't already have to support disadvantaged children to develop fluency of calculation?

Trust

- Do we talk about the things that really matter when it comes to maths?
- To what extent are you asked your opinion on important matters and decision-making regarding our maths curriculum or how we teach calculation and go about assessment?
- To what extent do leaders value dissenting views on how we teach and assess calculation?

Tim has these questions prepared but does not ask all of them. He keeps the conversation flowing, with the aim of building an accurate picture of the climate within the team. He resists the urge to add his own comments at first and shows that he is open to learning through how he introduces the issue:

Thanks for coming everyone. Today I'd like us to talk about maths, particularly the attainment of the least advantaged children and particularly the issue of their lack of fluency when calculating. It is an issue that is important for us to tackle because every child deserves the right support and one of the things that makes a big difference to how we teach, and therefore what children learn, is how we all feel about teaching maths. I'd like your feedback on a few things...

Tim asks some of these questions, summarising the responses and checking that he has accurately represented what others said. He picks up on a couple of themes:

- Colleagues felt that the maths curriculum was quite prescriptive with regard to the time to be spent on each topic, and felt under pressure to 'move on' to ensure coverage. They would like more autonomy to slow down and make sure that disadvantaged children understood what was being taught securely before moving on to another topic.
- Colleagues felt that there wasn't enough debate about how best to support disadvantaged children with low attainment to calculate effectively. Leaders seemed to have their preferred strategies.

With a better knowledge of the climate in the phase regarding supporting disadvantaged children to become more fluent when calculating, Tim now needs to know more about the systemic features of how teachers support the least advantaged in maths. He is aiming to improve teachers' feelings of autonomy and purpose around decision-making regarding when to move on through the sequence of maths lessons, as well as to build trust through encouraging debate. He decides to work on a *system* of better curriculum and teaching conversations in the team meetings (continued in Chapter 2).

Making a difference

Tim knows that these discussions are only the beginning and that bringing about systematic change will take time. In the meantime, he can still make a difference to the climate by continuing to pay attention to it in relation to the problem around maths. Continuing to talk about the things that matter (the experiences in maths of the least advantaged) slowly builds trust and firms up shared purpose. Continuing to seek feedback on the usefulness of the maths planning slowly builds trust and psychological safety through modelling the vulnerability necessary for a positive climate. Continuing to celebrate successes with the team when children do well, and drawing attention to how colleagues affect that success, increases the likelihood of flow and, again, reinforces purpose.

Example scenario: Senior leader

Background

Remember **Madiha**, the headteacher of a large primary school? She has a particular problem to solve with regard to improving reading attainment in Key Stage 2, despite children doing well with phonics and decoding.

Building knowledge of climate

Madiha wants to build her knowledge of the climate in the team regarding the teaching of reading, and sets aside a couple of weeks for lots of conversations, using the following as prompts:

Autonomy

- Tell me about the autonomy you have over how you teach reading.
- Tell me about the autonomy you have over how you assess and feed back in reading.
- Tell me about the autonomy you have over professional development regarding the teaching of reading.

Mastery and flow

- Do you get enough developmental feedback regarding the teaching of reading? What kind of feedback works best for you?
- What aspects of teaching reading do you feel good at? Are there any aspects of teaching reading that you do not feel good at?

Purpose

- What makes great teaching of reading?

Psychological safety

- To what extent have leaders been clear about what is expected in teaching reading?
- What training do you need in order to teach reading more effectively?

- What do you need that you don't already have to teach reading well?

Trust

- Do we talk about the things that really matter when it comes to reading?
- To what extent are you asked your opinion on important matters and decision-making regarding our reading curriculum or how we teach and assess?
- To what extent do leaders value dissenting views on how we teach and assess reading?

Madiha walks the school daily, noticing what colleagues are doing with reading, and selects from the prompts based on what she notices. She is careful to frame what she sees as a hypothesis to be tested, rather than absolute truth. For example:

> Thanks for popping in, Gene. I noticed today that you seemed a bit frustrated during reading and I want to help. It looked a bit to me like you felt that the lesson wasn't working; would that be fair to say?

Gene agrees. She talks about how she felt that there was much more to teaching reading in Year 3 than reading a passage and answering comprehension questions, which was the norm. Gene wants to try some of the things that she has read and heard about, such as focusing more on fluent reading, teaching vocabulary and background knowledge.

Madiha wants to know whether this is the case elsewhere in Key Stage 2, and continues meeting colleagues in groups to explore how they feel. Although others don't articulate what they want like Gene, Madiha picks up a combination of acceptance that reading is asking and answering comprehension questions and dissatisfaction that it is enough for some children but not for others. It is a similar situation in Year 2, but colleagues in Reception and Year 1 seem content with the phonics programme.

With a better knowledge of the climate in the phase regarding the teaching of reading, Madiha now needs to know more about the systemic features of how reading is actually taught. She aims to improve the team's feeling of autonomy and purpose around the teaching of reading. She decides to work on a *system* of developing a clear strategy with better professional development with regard to the teaching of reading beyond phonics (continued in Chapter 2), which also builds psychological safety and trust.

Making a difference

Affecting outcomes for children across the whole school will take time, but Madiha knows that she can influence the climate more immediately by continuing to pay attention to purpose, flow, autonomy, psychological safety and trust. Continuing to seek others' feedback on the emerging strategy demonstrates vulnerability, which is necessary for psychological safety and trust. Continuing to talk about reading with colleagues and encouraging experimentation establish shared purpose and autonomy.

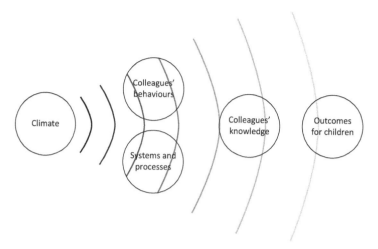

Figure 1.4 *How school climate influences the other impact domains.*

Leaders indirectly improve outcomes for children by giving status to colleagues' working conditions, allowing them to teach well day in, day out. Leaders can influence the extent to which colleagues feel autonomy over the work that they do, how they do it, when they do it and with whom they do it. Leaders can influence colleagues' feelings of mastery and purpose, as well as the levels of trust between them. Leaders can also influence the extent to which colleagues feel that they belong and their commitment to teaching, children, the school and change. Conversations yield information that is a good starting point for the important work of leadership – building an accurate picture of how colleagues feel about an issue and acting on those findings.

2 Systems and processes

You do not rise to the level of your goals. You fall to the level of your systems.

James Clear (2018, p. 27)

Why systems and processes matter

In Chapter 1, we explored the strong correlation between how a school runs (its established systems and processes) and how it feels for colleagues to work in that school. Leaders can make a difference to how colleagues feel about coming to work each day, and to outcomes for children, by attending to the systems and processes in the team or the school.

Essentially, schools do the same things – guide children through teachers and leaders' interpretation of the National Curriculum, over several years. It is how this complex work is organised that makes a difference to climate and, ultimately, to outcomes for children.

It has been documented that teachers working in more supportive professional environments improve their effectiveness more over time than teachers working in less supportive contexts, bucking the trend of a performance plateau after the first few years of teaching (Kraft and Papay, 2014). Kraft and Papay identified six aspects of strong professional development:

- consistently enforced rules around behaviour
- teachers given time and resources for professional development
- a culture of trust, respect and openness
- a commitment to student achievement
- opportunities for peer collaboration
- teacher evaluation based on improving the quality of teaching.

Expert leaders create or maintain systems in their phases, their subjects or their schools that enable consistently great teaching at scale, in an attempt to bring an element of order to the complexity of school life.

The components of systems and processes

Figure 2.1 *Common school systems and processes.*

Behaviour

Behaviour norms in a phase or around the school are a good example of the impact that leaders can have on systems and processes. This is the first indicator of Kraft and Papay's (2014) strong professional environment because it seeks to ensure that lessons are free from disruption so that children have a better chance of learning what is intended, and colleagues have a greater chance of enjoying their work. Behaviour systems are there to ensure that desired norms are promoted and that rules are consistently enforced in all aspects of school life, including in the classroom, the playground, the lunch hall and even on the journey to and from school.

An important and often overlooked part of a school's behaviour system is the equality of adult authority. In some schools, those with certain roles – such as teaching assistants, lunchtime controllers and colleagues who cover classes – can feel the brunt of poor behaviour. All schools will have a hierarchy of seniority, but children need to see all adults in the school as one – predictable in how they respond to desirable and undesirable behaviour and having the authority to lead groups of children. Leaders can influence this by empowering colleagues with clear behaviour strategies, regular training and actively seeking out the experiences of those whom children might perceive to have lower status. Leaders keen to help – and probably meaning well – who swoop in to deal with difficult behaviours that colleagues are experiencing can inadvertently reinforce a hierarchy. A more desirable approach in terms of long-term effectiveness for dealing with behaviour would be to coach and support colleagues through conversations with children, in order that they themselves are able to apply the strategies.

Professional development

The more leaders focus their relationships, their work and their learning on the core business of teaching and learning, the greater will be their influence on student outcomes.

Viviane Robinson (2011, p. 15)

Of all the areas on which leaders can focus, leading teacher learning and development has been found to make the greatest difference to outcomes for children (Robinson, 2011). Therefore, a vital system for leaders to establish is their professional development offer. Chapter 1 described how collective efficacy – the confidence that the team has in its ability to teach well and bring about good outcomes for children – is an important influence on climate, and that the professional development that leaders provide directly affects this. In addition, mastery is a key component of motivation, so leaders' systems must seek to support colleagues to get better over time at something that matters – teaching children well so that they learn the intended curriculum, as well as benefit from the pastoral outcomes described in Chapter 5.

There are several conditions for an effective professional development system (Cordingley et al., 2015):

- **duration:** at least two terms of multiple, iterative activities following initial input
- **rhythm:** frequent, meaningful engagement
- **relevance**: understand teachers' starting points and beliefs to generate buy-in
- **purpose:** ensure a positive professional environment, provide sufficient time
- **alignment:** use a variety of activities to reinforce messages
- **content:** prioritise subject knowledge, subject-specific pedagogy and formative assessment
- **activity:** explicit discussion on translating content to classroom – engage with evidence
- **collaboration:** work together towards a common goal to refine practice.

As well as conditions that must be systematic to support colleagues to improve, schools require drivers of professional development that enable them to engage with the content. The first driver is defining school strategies – a clear set of guidance, understood and enacted by all, on effective ways to go about teaching maths, managing behaviour, assessing what children have learned and so on. An example of the active ingredients that might be included in a maths strategy can be seen in Figure 2.2.

Maths strategy	Active ingredients
⊘ Daily review	⊘ Depth tasks for quick graspers
⊘ Worked examples and guided practice	⊘ Fluency/automaticity of facts and procedures
⊘ Scaffolded tasks for novices	⊘ Reasoning and problem solving throughout
⊘ Sufficient time to work without scaffolds	⊘ Concrete, pictorial and abstract representations

Figure 2.2 *Active ingredients of a school's maths strategy.*

There is plenty of evidence about effective maths strategies, but leaders have to be careful. If introducing a system that is too rigid, such as 'every lesson begins with ten minutes of retrieval practice', any gains might be offset by a feeling of a lack of autonomy. However, having clear core subject strategies can help to reduce the variability of experience that children in different classes receive.

> … it doesn't make that much difference what school you go to, but it matters very much which teachers you get in that school. If you get one of the best teachers you will learn in six months what it takes an average teacher a whole year to teach you. If you get one of the worst teachers, the same learning will take you over two years. There is a four-fold difference between the best and the worst teachers in the speed of student learning created.
>
> Dylan Wiliam (2006)

Systematic, high-quality professional development is needed to reduce any variability in the standard of teaching across the school, so that every child experiences the same quality of teaching, no matter which class or phase they are in.

Another driver of professional development is the system that we set up for colleagues to collaborate. Teachers are entitled to ten per cent of their timetable set aside for planning, preparation and assessment, and this regular time can be an important lever for improving teaching. When colleagues discuss, share knowledge and challenge ideas, they all benefit from a collective expertise, so sharing planning is a way in which to reduce variability for those schools fortunate enough to have multiple teachers in one year group. Colleagues' time is precious – even more so the time they have together – and sometimes this can be wasted. For example, having just over two hours a week together and using the time to decide what to teach, scrabbling around on teacher websites for resources, does not require the team to be together; instead, it creates a situation where colleagues work alongside each other, rather than with each other. A simple system whereby the expectation is that planning for the week ahead is done in advance and that meeting time set aside is used to talk through what will be taught, as well as how, sets colleagues up to benefit from the deep thinking that each team member will have carried out for the subjects that they have planned.

Curriculum

Since the curriculum is what leaders intend for children to learn, the systems that are established for how this learning happens will make a significant difference to successful implementation. A well-designed curriculum that is translated into a sequence of lessons is one of the most important systems that a school has, and yet there are many ways in which leaders can decide to do this. Consider two extreme examples:

A

Leaders provide colleagues with topic names on a whole-school overview. Colleagues then decide what they will teach in that unit, drawing in different subjects, often relying on resource websites to look for activities for children to do.

B

Leaders provide a detailed sequence of lessons for a given unit of work in each subject, including specifying the substantive knowledge that children should learn, the concepts that are built on from previous units of work and the disciplinary knowledge to be developed. Medium-term plans are written by subject experts for colleagues to work from.

There are advantages and disadvantages to both scenarios, and of course many variations between the extremes. In scenario A, workload is high, as colleagues are asked to do the curriculum design themselves. Even if they have had sufficient training to do this, multiple colleagues working on units of work in different year groups in a given subject can lead to a disjointed curriculum, where one unit of work bears no relation to the next. The topic-based approach can lead to blurring of conceptual understanding of what a subject is, resulting in children not knowing what 'history' is, for example. Scenario A does, however, afford teachers autonomy over what they are teaching, and the cross-curricular approach could result in children making connections between concepts in different subjects.

In scenario B, workload is lower as the curriculum design is carried out by a small number of colleagues with expertise, making it cohesive and well-sequenced. The distinction between subjects could help children to make important differentiations within those subjects, particularly in relation to the disciplinary knowledge. Scenario B does, however, limit colleagues' autonomy over what they teach and could result in children not making valid connections between units of work.

Whatever systems leaders settle on to translate curriculum overviews into teachable units of work, there will be a tension between workload and autonomy – two competing climate considerations.

Assessment

Fundamentally, the purpose of assessment is to find out what children have learned and, at scale, to ascertain the effectiveness of our curriculum and teaching. The systems that leaders implement to check the extent that children have learned the intended curriculum require careful thought. Educational assessment of years gone by involved attainment levels, assessment grids and teacher assessment – an incredible amount of work rooted in inevitable bias. What frequently emerged from the disbanding of attainment levels was all too similar – often just rebranded as working towards the expected standard, the expected standard and exceeding the expected standard, none of which are easily defined and often are simply there to try to demonstrate that children have made progress. Leaders might choose to monitor whether children are making progress by requesting teachers to complete several data drops per year and getting them to analyse that data, which takes away their time from two much better activities: thinking through curriculum content and day-to-day responsive teaching, based on what children seem to understand or don't understand.

Testing

Testing is an opportunity for leaders and teachers to build their knowledge of what children might have learned. There are countless providers of test papers to choose from, but the testing suite that leaders choose and how they implement it has a ripple effect across the school because of the nuances of assessment. An off-the-shelf assessment from a publisher is almost certainly not matched to the school's curriculum and therefore cannot systematically give teachers information about the extent to which children have learned what they have been taught. Combine that unreliable data with the time it takes to administer, mark and input data onto a tracking system and the result is a huge drain on colleagues' time for questionable benefit. That said, there are some options that could provide useful information with minimal workload implications. Tests that yield standardised scores can give an indication of broad attainment compared to national averages, which may be of use if leaders accept that they do not reflect what has been learned or not learned from the school's curriculum. Online tests that are marked instantly reduce unnecessary workload. Some might argue that the process of marking the test helps to understand what children can and can't do, and what they do and don't understand, but this is just what teachers do day in, day out, with a (hopefully) well-sequenced curriculum, so repeating this with random questions from a test paper seems an unnecessary distraction.

Marking and feedback

The system that leaders establish for checking children's work needs careful thought. Teachers obviously should be checking the work that children produce and using that information to provide feedback to children and to adapt upcoming plans. Somewhere along the line, schools seem to have settled on the least efficient way of doing this, with marking policies insisting on extensive written comments for every child that can only work if the child can a) read what the teacher has written, b) understand what the feedback means and c) be given time to read and act on it. For very young children, this is simply a waste of time. At its worst, written feedback might look like this:

- It might take three minutes to read, decide on feedback and write the feedback for each piece of work. That's 90 minutes for a class of 30 children.

- Then it might take another 15 minutes to return the books to the children and get them to act on the written feedback.

- If every child does exactly as the teacher intended, that's an hour and 45 minutes of work based on one task that might have taken less than an hour to do in the first place.

What's an alternative?

- It might take a minute for one teacher to scan a piece of work – half an hour in total.

- Then it will maybe take another 15 minutes to think through any common things to celebrate or improve. That's 45 minutes – half the time it took for writing a comment in every book.

- The next day it might take about ten minutes to tell the class what they did brilliantly, explain what they could do to improve and give them time to act on that advice, while nipping around to individuals who need more attention.

- That's still less than an hour and much less time than writing in every single book.

Quality assurance

Leaders need to know the reality of what is happening in classrooms every day in order to tailor professional development and bring about iterative improvement. Common mechanisms for quality assurance are lesson observations, learning walks and book scrutinies, and the challenge for leaders is to gather useful information without negatively affecting workload or climate. A theme throughout this book is the argument for inquiring into the reality of school life in each impact domain, avoiding the temptation to make judgements, building our knowledge so that we can make decisions that are more informed. In this sense, the five-part framework for making a difference described in this book is a form of quality assurance – a framework for building knowledge about related impact domains.

Should systems and processes be evaluated?

Systems are mass behaviours and leaders should definitely be knowledgeable about the behaviours that are systemic in their phase or across the whole school. Making an impact at scale relies on leaders designing and maintaining effective systems. Only by building knowledge of the reality of those systems and how they are affecting the other impact domains can leaders act and seek to influence adjustments to improve them.

Building knowledge of systems and processes

Leaders need to notice common behaviours within the school. What do colleagues do when presented with challenging behaviour? How do they prevent this? How do colleagues scaffold difficult tasks in maths? How do they teach writing? Leaders could check on the extent to which the systems that they have designed are actually happening but, even if they are, this is only the first step towards the ultimate desired impact of outcomes for children, so leaders must be careful not to declare success too early.

Behaviour

Leaders might build knowledge of the extent to which colleagues are doing the things that they have selected to tackle problems, but this has to be considered alongside outcomes for children. Regarding behaviour, for example, teachers or leaders could record the number of negative incidents. Of course, a lack of recording does not mean that negative behaviour isn't happening; any information relies on teachers a) being aware of such negative behaviour, b) intervening as appropriate and c) recording it.

Curriculum

When teaching the curriculum, the ultimate goal is for children to have learned what was planned for, but it is not easy to know for certain whether children have learned what was intended, as discussed previously in this chapter. Leaders must be cautious not to make invalid judgements about what children have learned based on the information that assessment practices might yield.

It is fairly common for leaders to look at the written work that children produce in order to make judgements on the quality of education, and doing so has its merits, but leaders need to understand what work in books can and cannot reliably tell them. For example, just because a child has completed some work in their book, does not mean that they have learned that content. Completing a task in a lesson where the teacher has just explained something is not evidence of learning, because learning happens over time and is different to performance.

Leaders might also look for how work changes over time. It is obvious to any observer if a child's handwriting is becoming neater over weeks and months and, looking more closely, it is also clear if their understanding of punctuation is improving. Comparisons of key concepts like this over time is far more useful for observing progress than considering the work produced in one lesson.

Another consideration that leaders must take into account when looking at written work is independence. Very often, work completed in books is not independent, because good teaching pushes children to work in their zone of proximal development. If children were working independently all of the time, teachers wouldn't be teaching them anything! Therefore, all that books really show leaders is the work that has been covered (although it could be that not all of this is in the books) and the standards of effort and presentation that colleagues accept.

Quality assurance

Lesson observations, where leaders watch a lesson and try to judge how good the teaching is or the extent of children's learning, are notoriously unreliable.

Using Ofsted's categories, if a lesson is judged 'Outstanding' by one observer, the probability that a second observer would give a different judgement is between 51% and 78%.

… fewer than 1% of those judged to be 'Inadequate' are genuinely inadequate; of those rated 'Outstanding', only 4% actually produce outstanding learning gains; overall, 63% of judgements will be wrong.

Professor Rob Coe (2014)

Quite simply, leaders cannot tell the quality of education from watching teaching, and if the process adds to colleagues' workload while negatively influencing climate, it is hard to see a benefit of doing lesson observations. Are learning walks a better system? It depends. If they are simply multiple lesson observations all at once, then no.

There is certainly value in leaders frequently visiting classrooms to build their knowledge of what is systematic. Seeing the reality of how children behave, how colleagues introduce new concepts and how children go about their work all contributes to leaders' knowledge of how the school runs. The information gathered can be used to get an idea of how systemic chosen strategies are. For example, is vocabulary explicitly taught? Are teachers checking for understanding? However, it is too easy for leaders to walk around with a clipboard checking for compliance. Compliance does not necessarily mean impact, although it certainly could be a start. Yes, leaders may have settled on the active ingredients of strategies for teaching English, or managing behaviour, or supporting children with SEND, for example, but what matters is the difference that those strategies make to children.

Talking with colleagues about what they are teaching and talking with children about what they have learned can bring context to what leaders see (or don't see) around the school. But no system of quality assurance can support leaders to make inferences that are absolute truth – rather, they will be hunches that require exploration.

To simplify the evaluation of systems, leaders might decide to have plenty of conversations about how the school runs with a cross-section of colleagues. Mowles suggests as much in his book *Complexity:*

There is no communication so clear and no rule so precise that it won't need exploring and repeating before the manager and the managed have a good enough understanding of what is intended.

Chris Mowles (2021, p. 176)

No matter the level of thought that has gone into designing a system for behaviour, professional learning, curriculum planning or quality assurance, once it is implemented all manner of unexpected snags will become apparent, and the only way to truly discover them is to regularly talk to those colleagues experiencing them.

What could we do with the knowledge that we've built about systems and processes?

Using the knowledge that has been built in relation to systems and processes is vital. If leaders are evaluating what is systemic across the school, their response should be systemic too. It would be tempting to zero in on individual colleagues, providing them with personal feedback, but leaders must consider what is contributing to the systemic features of school life. The knowledge built in relation to a school system should lead to actions for *leaders*, not individuals. Does professional development need to improve? For whom? Does communication need to be clearer or more timely?

Example scenario: Middle leader

Background

Remember **Tim**, a lower Key Stage 2 phase leader in a two-form-entry primary school? He has a particular problem to solve around improving fluency of calculation for disadvantaged children in Year 3 and Year 4.

After inquiring into climate, Tim found that colleagues felt under pressure to 'move on' to ensure coverage and wanted more autonomy to slow down and make sure that disadvantaged children understood what was being taught. They also wanted more debate about how best to support disadvantaged children to improve their fluency of calculation.

Building knowledge of systems and processes

Tim now needs to know more about what is systemic in the teaching of calculation and supporting the least advantaged across the phase, and so spends time observing what is happening in lessons and talking to colleagues about the decisions that they are making. Tim notices that teachers often explain concepts to the whole class well enough, but don't check the understanding of the least advantaged or engage them much in any shared problem-solving, instead taking the responses from a few children as an indicator that it is time to move on. Teaching assistants often support the least advantaged while they work and prompt them to 'get the work done', rather than prioritising their understanding.

Tim designs a system for providing prompts in team meetings in order for the team to:

- discuss the most appropriate form of support for the least advantaged
- establish some rules of thumb for when to move on to the next lesson in the sequence or to spend more time consolidating understanding (continued in Chapter 3).

Making a difference

Tim knows that systems make a difference because they can keep colleagues focused on the shared purpose. They are shared practices, not individual behaviours (although they are dependent on the actions of individuals). Therefore, Tim knows that the way in which he runs team meetings is the important driver for making a difference. He continues to raise the issue of support for the least advantaged in every team meeting, and expects colleagues to talk about it too. He continues to model his own thinking about when he is moving on to the next lesson in the sequence and when he is not, encouraging others to also share their reasoning.

Example scenario: Senior leader

Background

Remember **Madiha**, the headteacher of a large primary school? She has a particular problem to solve in relation to improving reading attainment in Key Stage 2, despite children doing well with phonics and decoding.

After inquiring into the climate, she found that there was a mixture of contentment and dissatisfaction with how reading was taught.

Building knowledge of systems and processes

Madiha now needs to know more about what is systemic in the teaching of reading. She notices that, often, teachers will find a text with already prepared comprehension questions from a teacher resource website. These exercises will not be adapted in any way and teachers set them in reading lessons a few times per week. During these lessons, teachers get children to read the text to themselves and then answer the questions, after which the children mark their own work. Madiha notices that the only discussion about reading that takes place during team meetings is sharing the comprehension sheets that have been chosen.

Madiha designs a system of professional development based on a clearer strategy for teaching reading beyond phonics, including using team meetings as a driver for conversations (continued in Chapter 3).

Making a difference

Madiha knows that systems contribute to how colleagues feel and are therefore vital for a positive climate. With team meetings being a driver for supporting colleagues to understand their emerging strategy, she continues to talk regularly with phase leaders about the kinds of things that each team needs to focus on when they get together. These include areas such as continuing to develop the active ingredients involved in the planning of reading, which they have been working on as a team. Madiha also understands that it is easy for teams to slip back into old habits, so she continues to talk to phase leaders about guarding against the re-emergence of comprehension sheets and simply answering questions about a text.

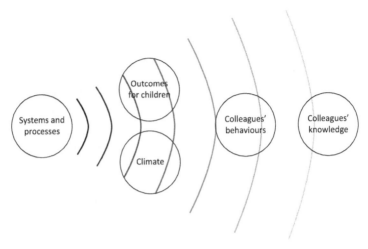

Figure 2.3 *How systems and processes influence the other impact domains.*

Colleagues continue to improve if they work in a strong professional environment that comprises the systems that leaders establish. Good behaviour systems allow colleagues to teach and children to learn. Prioritising professional development with well-thought-out systems is necessary to bring about improvement in outcomes for children. Leaders need to make deliberate choices to manage the tension between workload and autonomy in many systems, while ensuring that they are efficient in order to allow colleagues plenty of time for those tasks that they regularly need to carry out that matter the most. Systems for quality assurance must provide useful information without adversely affecting staff climate.

3 Colleagues' knowledge

*The most effective teachers have a deep knowledge of the
subjects that they teach.*

Coe et al. (2014, p. 2)

Why colleagues' knowledge matters

Knowledge is the prerequisite for any effective teaching. Colleagues
will not be able to explain concepts clearly, check understanding,
give incisive feedback or manage behaviour well without knowing
a great deal about these things. We design and maintain systems in
our team or in our school to improve practice and influence what
children learn. But these systems can only have an impact if all those
who are part of the system have extensive knowledge of what they
are doing and why. Actions are dependent on knowledge; therefore,
leaders need to inquire into colleagues' mental models (the
knowledge that they have and how that knowledge is organised)
to enable them to act upon it. Leaders can then support colleagues
to develop broader and better connected mental models, in order to
bring about improvement.

The components of colleagues' knowledge

Knowledge is more than facts or theory. It can be organised into
two types:

- **Formal knowledge** is universal and can be easily stated and
  shared. Insights from research into cognitive science provide an
  example of formal knowledge.

- **Hidden knowledge** is contextual:
  - knowledge learned from experiences
  - knowledge connected to feelings, values or moods (often referred to as intuition)
  - knowledge of how to manage our own performance (Bereiter and Scardamalia, 1993).

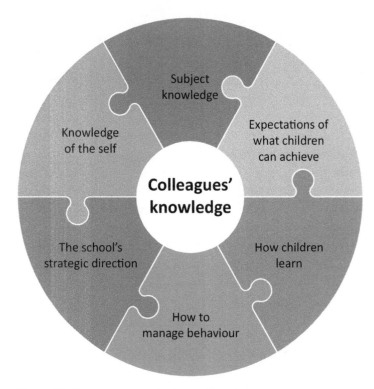

Figure 3.1 *The components of colleagues' knowledge.*

Subject knowledge

Colleagues need sufficient formal subject knowledge, which is made up of a number of components (Coe et al., 2014):

- knowledge of the content being taught,
- knowledge of how best to teach the content and
- knowledge of common misconceptions and when they are likely to occur.

Subject content refers to much more than simply the content to be taught. It includes the curriculum knowledge of the position of what is being taught in the overall sequence of learning – what children will have learned before that is being built upon, as well as what will be coming later on that the current work is preparing them for.

Then there is pedagogical knowledge. This includes more general knowledge about how one might explain clearly, get children thinking deeply about concepts or check for understanding. It also includes content-specific pedagogical knowledge, such as effective ways in which to model a writer's thought processes or to work out fractions of amounts. For each topic in a curriculum, there will be useful knowledge for effectively teaching it.

Finally, there is knowledge of common misconceptions and when they are likely to occur. Colleagues with extensive knowledge of the subject content that they are teaching will know at which points children run into difficulty with conceptual understanding. This will enable them to pre-empt those misconceptions or to deal with them effectively when they arise.

A vast amount of subject knowledge requirements would be classified as formal, but there are examples of valuable and relevant hidden knowledge that we might seek to influence. While the Sutton Trust report identifies knowledge of common misconceptions (Coe et al., 2014), even more important for colleagues are the actual, specific misconceptions of the children that they are supporting. The context of the school and children's experiences in previous years may have resulted in a unique pattern of misconceptions that would be incredibly valuable for colleagues to know. For example, a class with a previous teacher that had weaker subject knowledge might have misconceptions around sentence-level grammar. Disrupted schooling, as seen in the coronavirus pandemic, could also be a significant influence on a cohort's misconceptions.

Expectations of what children can achieve

Useful knowledge for colleagues is what excellent work looks like for the tasks that they are setting. Without this knowledge, opportunities to challenge children who could do better may be missed. Seeing what children are capable of doing in different classes, subjects or year groups can help to calibrate what colleagues might expect.

How children learn

Great teaching is ensuring that children learn what is intended; therefore, colleagues need good knowledge of how children learn.

> *Learning is a change in long term memory.*
>
> Kirschner et al. (2006, p. 75)

Taking Kirschner et al.'s (2006) definition of learning, colleagues would benefit from knowing about the difference between working memory and long-term memory, as well as how information is encoded into and retrieved from long-term memory. If colleagues know the difference between working and long-term memory, it is also then useful to know about cognitive load theory and the limitations of working memory, because these have significant implications for what colleagues can do to avoid overloading children. This links with desirable pedagogical knowledge, such as breaking down tasks into small chunks, but also leads colleagues down the route of needing to know about attention. If working memory is where children think (and they remember what they think about), colleagues need to plan their learning environment so as not to undermine their efforts to teach. For example, an overly busy classroom with every inch of wall space covered with some poster or other provides a huge amount of information for children to pay attention to that could compete with what the teacher actually wants them to pay attention to. Knowing this is vital in order for colleagues to make informed decisions that affect learning.

What is also useful for colleagues to know are the mechanisms around motivation, because knowing them enables more effective practice. Children are more likely to be motivated if they:

- feel successful
- know and engage in routines
- see other children working hard
- feel like they belong
- have committed to working hard (Mccrea, 2020).

The significance of deliberately seeking to influence what colleagues know cannot be understated. After all, they will not be able to enact new or improved pedagogy without first knowing what it is.

How to manage behaviour

It is vital that colleagues know the intricacies of the school's strategies to promote good behaviour, prevent bullying and ensure that children complete assigned work, in order to establish consistent application across classes, year groups and key stages. And of course, this knowledge is a prerequisite to them actually enacting those strategies. Clearly, the better that colleagues understand the expectations relating to behaviour and the systems used to ensure that those expectations are met, the more likely that they will manage behaviour consistently and the better that behaviour will be. Through leaders' coaching, colleagues might know more about the benefits and drawbacks of extrinsic rewards, or they might develop a growing understanding of school suspensions and exclusions because of invitations to shadow decision-making. Knowledge of how to lead behaviour is an important difference that we can make because colleagues will not be able to implement chosen strategies unless they know what they are and understand the reasoning behind them.

Formal knowledge is essential for colleagues to enable them to manage behaviour effectively, but alone it is insufficient. There is also a wealth of hidden knowledge that leaders will want colleagues to know. It would be desirable for individuals to build up informal knowledge from previously encountered experiences. For example:

- Is there a particular lesson, location or point in the term where managing behaviour in this class requires more careful planning and more skilful execution?
- What is the most effective furniture arrangement for different activities to support this class to maintain focus?
- Which combinations of children sitting together work well and which need to be avoided?
- Do some children respond better to a stern word or a quiet reminder?
- For which children does talking to their parents help when something goes wrong?
- Do some children need regular breaks from the stimulation of the classroom?
- Everyone has biases, so do colleagues treat different groups of children in different ways?

The school's strategic direction

All colleagues should have a good knowledge of the school's strategic direction, because when they do, it enables collective action towards that objective. The collective sense of purpose, which is part of the climate impact domain, can only happen when each individual develops their own understanding of it. In Chapter 1, we were introduced to a model for thinking about strategic direction, but the shared purpose that is desirable is dependent on colleagues' understanding of the model, as can be seen in Figure 3.2.

School improvement model

Aim	For what purpose does this school exist?
Values	What behaviours make us unique?
Vision	What is the future ideal for how the school runs?
Strategic priorities	What specific problems require our attention to realise our vision?
Drivers	What systems will help to address strategic priorities?
Strategies and their active ingredients	What strategies are required and what are the key concepts and behaviours that need to be implemented for them to be successful?

Figure 3.2 *A model for school improvement that supports leaders to define purpose.*

Without this shared knowledge, the work of individuals would inevitably be disjointed. It may be that some colleagues have a limited understanding of the school's strategic priorities, or that other colleagues can remember the school values when prompted but don't actively make decisions with them in mind. There may be colleagues who are able to talk about some of the active ingredients of the school's behaviour strategy but have forgotten other equally important ones.

Knowledge of the self

Leaders can make a difference to what colleagues know of themselves, and this in turn can help them to develop their practice. A good starting point is to ensure that colleagues have an idea of their strengths and areas for improvement, although, as discussed previously, making an accurate judgement of effective teaching is very difficult. What might be more useful is to help colleagues to recognise any biases. We all have biases because we are human; they manifest in the attention that we give others, the warmth of interactions, what we expect others to be capable of and the quality of feedback that we offer. For some, this works out positively when our expectations are high, but the opposite is also true. It is probably unavoidable that we have lower expectations of some, demonstrating it through less attention, colder interactions and poorer feedback. If it is possible to change our biases, knowing them is a logical first step. Leaders can, for example, point out which children are called upon to speak most often or point out the quality of feedback given to different children. Colleagues may not realise how such bias manifests; this is explored more in Chapter 4.

Should colleagues' knowledge be evaluated?

Given that any adoption of new teaching behaviours or refinement of existing behaviours is predicated on knowledge, leaders need to know what their colleagues know. Prior knowledge is surely one of the most important factors in what colleagues are capable of learning. Implementing a school-wide approach to teaching or behaviour, or any other aspect of education, is made or broken on colleagues' understanding. Leaders need a sound understanding of what individuals know, as well as the collective, shared understanding that the team has. Making judgements about what colleagues understand is unnecessary. We need only to gain insights into what they already know in order to support them in building their knowledge to a standard necessary to take informed action and contribute to the systems that we have designed.

Building knowledge of colleagues' mental models

Leaders can make inferences from colleagues' actions or, preferably, bring their mental models (what they know and how it is organised) to life by engaging in conversations about things that matter. The most sensible way of building knowledge of what colleagues know would be to use the natural outputs of their day-to-day work and have regular conversations with them about both the headlines and the detail, paying attention to:

- planned sequences of lessons, and the quality and clarity of explanations
- the way in which work is scaffolded and the feedback that is given to children if they do not understand
- how they interact with children
- how they set up their classroom
- the expectations that they set out
- how they challenge sub-standard effort.

Inquiry into all of these aspects of school life will reveal colleagues' subject knowledge, including in relation to how children learn, as well as their understanding of the school's strategic direction and what requires collective attention in order to bring about improvement.

Although building knowledge of what colleagues know is a useful endeavour for leaders, the way in which we choose to do so will affect school climate. Done inconsiderately, it could negatively affect the climate in school; done well, it could amplify the sense of purpose and mastery that colleagues feel. Poorly carried-out lesson observations or work scrutiny can damage trust, which might far outweigh the potential benefits of what leaders learn from the process.

What could we do with the knowledge that we've built about colleagues' mental models?

Any information gathered on what colleagues know needs to inform professional development plans. If colleagues have incomplete understanding of particular concepts, or if they have misconceptions, then leaders should seek to address these through the school's professional development systems. Viviane Robinson's theory of action (2017) suggests that behaviours (in this case, how colleagues teach and support children) are sustained by beliefs, attitudes and values. She advocates that the target of change should not be what colleagues do, but what they believe and value. Naturally, what colleagues know influences the formation of these beliefs and values; therefore, professional development systems must prioritise improving colleagues' understanding of the school's strategic direction. They must give colleagues the opportunity to develop formal knowledge related to subjects, how children learn, expectations of what is possible and how to manage behaviour. And they must also support colleagues to develop ways of understanding informal knowledge – specific misconceptions and support strategies that seem to work with the children that they teach. Simply mandating behaviour change is insufficient.

Example scenario: Middle leader

Background

Remember **Tim**, a lower Key Stage 2 phase leader in a two-form-entry primary school? He has a particular problem to solve around improving fluency of calculation for disadvantaged children in Year 3 and Year 4.

After inquiring into the climate, Tim found that colleagues felt under pressure to 'move on' to ensure coverage and wanted more autonomy to slow down and make sure that disadvantaged children understood what was being taught. They also wanted more debate about how best to support disadvantaged children to improve their fluency of calculation.

After inquiring into what was systemic in their teaching of maths across the phase, Tim noticed that teachers often explained concepts to the whole class well enough but didn't check the understanding of the least advantaged or engage them much in any shared examples, instead taking the responses from a few children as an indicator that it was time to move on. Teaching assistants often supported the least advantaged while they worked and prompted them to 'get the work done' rather than prioritising their understanding.

Building knowledge of colleagues' mental models

Tim designs a system for providing prompts in team meetings in order for the team to:

- discuss the most appropriate form of support for the least advantaged
- establish some rules of thumb for when to move on to the next lesson in the sequence or to spend more time consolidating understanding.

First, though, Tim needs to know more about the team's underlying beliefs and their shared mental model of great maths teaching. He uses some team meeting time to satisfy the team's need for debate and to uncover what they know, by presenting some statements and asking what they think:

- We should set children for maths rather than have mixed attainment classes.
- Children need to use concrete manipulatives in every lesson.
- A clear explanation and thorough modelling is the best form of scaffolding.
- We should teach to the top and scaffold.
- During each lesson, all children can be working on the same objective.

The team enjoy the conversations, which continue informally over the following days. Tim develops an understanding that, although there is a strong collective agreement on what is involved in a good explanation of typical calculations, teachers are stumped as to how to support the least advantaged children when there are so many gaps in their knowledge. Tim also decides to explore the team's understanding of maximising children's attention and finds that although there is an acceptance that children should concentrate, many of the least advantaged children struggle with this.

To enable his team meeting system to succeed, Tim sets a weekly task to read a blog post or extract from a book on topics such as reducing cognitive load, explicitly checking and teaching prerequisite knowledge, the arguments for and against setting, and task design with scaffolding. Meetings start with a review of what everyone has read and then Tim encourages the team to commit to trying something different, based on the topics that the team has read about (continued in Chapter 4).

Making a difference

Tim knows that what his colleagues understand about key issues to do with maths and the least advantaged children has to be prioritised before expecting any improvements in practice, and so he keeps up the momentum of sharing what they are all learning. After setting the team short reading tasks, he encourages connections with previously discussed concepts by modelling this himself and prompting colleagues to consider: *How does what we've discussed about the arguments for and against setting relate to what we talked about last time regarding checking and teaching prerequisite knowledge before a unit of work begins?* He also encourages the sharing of related articles and books. Side conversations with individuals often result in recommendations for further reading on a subject that he has prepared in advance.

Background

Remember **Madiha**, the headteacher of a large primary school? She has a particular problem to solve about improving reading attainment in Key Stage 2, despite children doing well with phonics and decoding.

After inquiring into the climate, Madiha found that there was a mixture of contentment and dissatisfaction with how reading was taught.

After inquiring into teaching practices that were systemic, she noticed that often teachers would use resource websites to find stand-alone comprehension activities (a text and some questions) to set a few times a week. Children would simply read the text to themselves and then answer the questions. The only discussion of reading in team meetings was sharing the comprehension sheets that had been chosen.

Building knowledge of colleagues' mental models

Madiha designs a system of professional development based on a clearer strategy for teaching reading beyond phonics, including using team meetings as a driver for conversations. But first, she needs to inquire into the team's underlying beliefs about what makes great teaching of reading and what they know about how children get better at reading. She sets aside a couple of twilight sessions to generate discussion. In advance, she sends colleagues some links to articles to prompt their thinking, and encourages colleagues who were dissatisfied with how reading was taught to speak up when the time comes. Madiha ascertains that, in general, the collective understanding of reading includes:

- Reading at the end of Key Stage 2 is assessed by reading a text and answering questions, so it makes sense to practise that.
- Parents should be encouraging their children to read more at home.
- Some children with dyslexic tendencies will always find reading difficult.
- Getting better at reading requires lots of practice of skills, such as prediction and inference.

From her own research, Madiha knows the importance of focusing on fluency and prosody, the deliberate teaching of vocabulary and teaching relevant background knowledge, but most colleagues have not considered these and have limited knowledge of them.

To enable her professional development system to succeed, Madiha steers subsequent discussions towards forming a list of the active ingredients of a fledgling reading strategy – the concepts and behaviours that need to be present in order to improve the teaching of reading. She also provides examples from other schools of what a sequence of lessons might look like in a reading unit of work, and develops a shared understanding of how a unit would be structured in their school to incorporate these active ingredients. Finally, she wants to build the team's knowledge of great books by asking them to research and contribute to a reading spine on which they will build units of work. All this knowledge development enables teams to engage in planning and teaching in a new way (continued in Chapter 4).

Making a difference

Madiha knows that a clear set of active ingredients will be a great structure around which to develop colleagues' mental models of the teaching of reading. In the first instance, she prioritises supporting others' understanding of these active ingredients, and continues to refer to them in every conversation that she has about reading. She is very careful about her use of language so as to enable many shared conversations where she is confident that colleagues understand one another. The active ingredients of the reading strategy are:

- teach the background knowledge needed to understand the text
- vocabulary instruction
- model and practise fluency and prosody
- reading to children and oral comprehension
- model the reader's thought processes.

Madiha particularly prioritises conversations around these active ingredients with phase leaders because she wants team planning meetings to be an important driver in improving practice. The conversations that phase leaders have with their teams will be crucial in influencing practice and maintaining momentum.

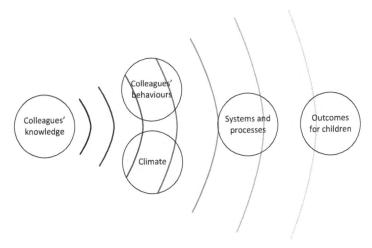

Figure 3.3 *How colleagues' knowledge influences the other impact domains.*

What colleagues know determines their behaviour in the classroom and when interacting with each other, and there are different types of knowledge that they should acquire. Formal knowledge is universal, but hidden knowledge is context-specific. Subject knowledge is vital for effective teaching, but it is much more than subject content and includes pedagogical knowledge and common misconceptions. Knowledge of how children learn affords better decision-making in the classroom, and if colleagues are to establish a purposeful classroom, they need knowledge of how to establish and maintain social norms as part of school policy. If colleagues understand and buy into the school's strategic direction, they are more likely to make a positive contribution to whole-school improvement. All of us have biases, and if we are to try to change them, knowing them is a logical first step.

4 Colleagues' behaviours

*Great teachers create a supportive environment for learning…
Great teachers manage the classroom to maximise the
opportunity to learn…*

*Great teachers present content, activities and interactions that
activate their students' thinking.*

Coe et al. (2020, pp. 22, 27, 30)

Why colleagues' behaviours matter

Clearly, the decisions that colleagues make in the classroom and
the actions that they take affect not only how children behave, but
also the extent to which they engage with lesson content. Plenty of
research into what makes great teaching identifies key behaviours
such as explaining concepts clearly, checking that children have
understood or giving timely and incisive feedback. These are more
than just skills; they are bound up with what colleagues know about
these behaviours, along with what they know about the children in
front of them. Chapter 3 described the importance of knowledge,
and this chapter explains the necessary next step – using that
knowledge to do something different or to adjust existing practice.
The behaviours of individual colleagues, when they become habitual,
turn into classroom systems and routines, and wider systems become
established when those behaviours are shared across a team or the
whole school.

The components of colleagues' behaviours

Figure 4.1 *The components of colleagues' behaviours.*

Expectations of children

We all have an expectation of what children are capable of and hold them to a set of standards based on those beliefs. Making a difference to the quality of teaching and classroom support can start by standardising what is expected of children – setting high but reasonable goals and encouraging children to respond positively to the challenge of these goals. If colleagues' beliefs about what children are capable of are combined with expert pedagogy, children are in a much better position to flourish.

The Pygmalion effect describes how teachers' expectations influence children's achievements (Rosenthal and Jacobsen, 1968). The researchers found that when teachers were led to expect high performance from children, regardless of current attainment, they treated them differently and the children succeeded – for example, by:

- paying closer attention to high-expectancy children
- spending more time with high-expectancy children
- giving high-expectancy children more and better-quality feedback.

The opposite effect was also seen – whereby children did not succeed – when teachers were led to expect low performance; with this comes the tricky problem of bias. We cannot avoid bias – it is human nature – but where this becomes problematic in teaching is when it leads to the soft bigotry of low expectations of children who are disadvantaged in some way. Low expectations might not be deliberate but examples include:

- failing to give feedback to responses from low-expectancy pupils
- criticising low-expectancy pupils more often
- not waiting as long for the answers of low-expectancy pupils
- calling on low-expectancy pupils less frequently to answer questions
- asking low-expectancy pupils only lower-order questions
- giving low-expectancy pupils low-level academic tasks
- leaving low-expectancy pupils out of some learning activities.

Biases might be hard to change, but if we are able to influence colleagues' mindsets about what children are capable of achieving, it can make a difference to their learning.

Colleagues' behaviours

Ensuring success

There is plenty of evidence to suggest the potentially most effective strategies that teachers could use to help children to succeed, such as presenting new material in small steps, checking children's understanding and providing scaffolds for difficult tasks. Supporting colleagues to refine these behaviours is at the heart of good professional development and improving outcomes for children. Great teaching requires understanding concepts such as reducing cognitive load by providing clear explanations, but such strategies need to be applied through responsive teaching, which includes setting clear learning goals, checking children's understanding and adapting teaching where necessary (Fletcher-Wood, 2018).

Children are more likely to be motivated if they experience success, and so great teaching enables children to feel successful. Mccrea (2020) suggests that explicitly describing what success looks like is the all-important first step, and colleagues may often have to work hard to change children's mindsets about what success is. Consider the example of a teacher praising a piece of writing by saying something along the lines of: *'Wow! Look at how much writing you've done!'* This communicates the idea that success is a lot of writing. Children may then prioritise filling a page with writing rather than carefully thinking through the content and accuracy. There is a similar trap with praising children for 'finishing all their work'. Here, the success is framed as task completion, but most colleagues can readily think of an example of a child having completed work even though they have not understood what has been taught. A significant impact that leaders can have on colleagues' behaviours might be to encourage the prioritisation of understanding over task completion.

As described earlier in the chapter, low expectations can be communicated by setting low-level tasks. Addressing this could involve setting higher-level tasks for all, but of course such tasks will need to be adapted in some way to enable everyone to access them. Encouraging colleagues to scaffold rather than give 'easier' work is therefore an important behaviour for us to influence, providing support to access challenging content and removing obstacles. Creating several different tasks for children to complete based on perceived ability not only reduces the thinking that some children are required to do, but also significantly increases workload for probably a net negative effect on children. The scaffolding strategies that leaders might want to see from colleagues include:

- breaking down tasks into smaller chunks
- allowing enough time to practise to automaticity
- giving sufficient time to process instructions and work on tasks
- presenting information in graphic organisers rather than dense text
- using concrete/pictorial representations
- carrying out oral rehearsal with an adult
- using partially completed examples
- using minimally different questions (variation theory).

All of these scaffolding strategies are designed to reduce the cognitive load of the tasks set so that children can experience success while still accessing challenging concepts. However, this is only the first stage. To use a building analogy, scaffolding is a temporary structure used to enable the important building work. Eventually it is removed, and the same idea needs to be applied to the scaffolding of tasks. Children must be given an opportunity to build automaticity and familiarity to the extent where they can demonstrate their understanding without the scaffolds.

Managing behaviour

The disciplinary climate in a classroom matters. When children come to school on time, follow rules and have good relationships with one another, there is less likely to be disruption or conflict and therefore children will be free to focus on learning. It is a prerequisite for great teaching and, as such, we should seek to provide continuous support for colleagues so that behaviour is not an issue in their classrooms. A colleague who expends all their attention on managing children's behaviour will have little capacity to enact effective pedagogy, so an important impact that leaders can have on individual colleagues is to support them to become experts in managing their classes.

The actions that colleagues take each day result in the classroom culture, and Mccrea (2020) suggests three strategies to influence the class's social norms:

- **Elevate visibility:** Ensure that as many children as possible are behaving in the desired way and that all children have memorable sightings of the behaviour.
- **Amplify approval:** Ensure that it is not just the adults that reinforce the desired behaviours but peers too.
- **North Star norms:** Have simple and easy-to-follow ways of behaving that involve the whole community.

How colleagues manage the third strategy, North Star norms, is important. Some, with the best intentions, come up with very long lists of rules that seem to grow in response to incidents, often prefixed with 'Don't'. Long lists of rules are hard to remember, and therefore leaders should look to influence how colleagues talk about their expectations.

Building relationships

Children follow people before they follow rules; relationships have to be good enough to breed trust if children are to make the most of the learning opportunities on offer. Children who feel like they belong are more motivated, and there are things that colleagues can do to influence this. Mccrea (2020) suggests:

- **Signal status:** Show that children belong to the group and include everyone.

- **Cultivate affinity:** Develop a shared identity and emphasise what everyone has in common.

- **Earn trust:** Show children care and be consistent.

Directing attention

If we want to control what our students learn, we've got to be intentional and specific about what they should be attending to. Not only do we need to orient attention, but we must do it with precision.

Peps Mccrea (2017, p. 39)

Children learn what they pay attention to, so colleagues who direct attention clearly are more likely to be successful in getting children to learn the intended curriculum. Put simply, colleagues should make it obvious what to look out for in advance, and then draw attention to that thing using gesture, voice or visuals. Prioritising how colleagues direct attention could be a fruitful strand of professional development.

Engagement in professional development

Every teacher needs to improve, not because they are not good enough, but because they can be even better.

Dylan Wiliam (2012)

Schools may well have a great system for professional development, but what matters is the extent to which each colleague engages with it. There is never enough time in the working week, but supporting colleagues to free up some time to develop themselves, by stopping or reducing less important behaviours, is a behaviour change that we can influence. If a colleague is better read or having more discussions, seeking out ways in which to improve their practice as a result of our actions, then a significant difference has been made.

Efficiency in core tasks

There are certain tasks that colleagues carry out repeatedly, and the most significant of these is lesson planning. Early career teachers will often spend many hours planning lessons that will last a lot less time than that spent planning them, but over time they will become more efficient. This is something to continually strive for because the more autonomous teachers are at planning, the more attention they can devote to other aspects of teaching. There are two elements to becoming more efficient. The first concerns content and lesson design – selecting models, explanations, tasks and scaffolds that will help children to learn what is intended. The second concerns the technical aspects of planning, such as use of IT in preparing what children will see in lessons. Both of these take hours each week, but leaders can make a difference by sharing hacks, such as shortcuts for common programmes used for planning, and by removing barriers, such as providing reliable IT equipment.

Should colleagues' behaviours be evaluated?

Making a judgement about the quality of what colleagues do is subject to flaws in reasoning. Ultimately, whether colleagues' behaviours are any good is dependent on the result of those behaviours – are children learning better or behaving better? In complex classrooms, though, it is folly to think that we can determine causation when there are so many possible factors involved – and that is assuming that we can make valid judgements on what children have learned.

This can contribute to a problematic situation where confirmation bias kicks in. If we have advocated for a particular strategy and we notice some successes, it is human nature to attribute those successes to the behaviour that we have influenced. In reality, it is almost impossible to know. We might then fall into the trap of just looking for the prevalence of whatever it is that we want colleagues to do. This is how fads take hold; leaders give status to a particular behaviour and colleagues conform by demonstrating it. The reality could well be that the only time those behaviours are carried out is when the leader is watching!

As for all of the impact domains, making judgements on quality is less useful than building knowledge of what colleagues routinely do. Accurate knowledge of such habits allows us to genuinely support colleagues to reflect on their developing understanding of what they are doing and why, the effect of their working practices on how they are feeling and, ultimately, how children are responding.

Building knowledge of colleagues' behaviours

The methods for building knowledge of systems and processes described in Chapter 2 are the same for building knowledge of the behaviour of individual colleagues, with a shift in focus to the individual. Noticing the details of what colleagues do in given situations is an important accompaniment to exploring their understanding and beliefs, as described in the previous chapter. However, visiting lessons should be treated with the same caution as discussed in Chapter 2. Even just being in the room can affect the decisions that colleagues make, so what we observe can never be considered in isolation.

While the approaches to building knowledge described in Chapter 2 support our understanding of collective behaviours and general patterns, we need to shift our focus to specific behaviours for individuals – the more specific, the better. Inquiring into systems might be broader, such as: What do they do when presented with challenging behaviour? How do they prevent it? How do they scaffold difficult tasks in maths? How do they teach writing? But inquiring into individuals' behaviours can be more granular:

- What do they do when child X interrupts or strays off task? How do they prevent it?
- How do they scaffold difficult tasks involving calculation for child Y in maths?
- How do they give feedback when children read robotically or miss punctuation marks?

There is some room for measurement when it comes to behaviours, particularly in the realm of addressing bias. For example, if we know the behaviours that communicate low expectations, and colleagues are engaged with the idea of identifying their biases, a technique such as counting the frequency and length of interactions with certain children might provide an opportunity for colleagues to address their biases.

What could we do with the knowledge that we've built about colleagues' behaviours?

While building knowledge of systemic behaviours results in actions for leaders, building knowledge of individuals' behaviours should result in actions for colleagues, enabled by leaders. Any information gathered about what colleagues do should be with the intention of improving those behaviours. We might seek to help them to make explanations of mathematical concepts more precise. We might look to support them in improving their presence in the classroom by adding gestures or adjusting positioning in the classroom. We might seek to support colleagues to make feedback clearer or more timely when children read without expression. Coaching conversations about improving an aspect of practice can be followed up by deliberate, collaborative planning between colleague and leader to address the area for improvement.

It is helpful for leaders to understand how habits form and to use this knowledge to support colleagues. A simple model of habit forming includes a cue, a response and a reward. The cue needs to be planned for because it triggers the response (in our case, the behaviour that we are supporting colleagues to develop). The reward makes us feel good enough to want to repeat the response. Let us consider an example of a leader supporting a colleague to give clear feedback when a child reads without expression:

- The cue is robotic reading.

- The response might be to stop the child, model expressive reading and then ask them to mimic.

- The reward is the child reading with expression and the success that both the colleague and the child experience.

Example scenario: Middle leader

Background

Remember **Tim**, a lower Key Stage 2 phase leader in a two-form-entry primary school? He is seeking to solve a problem around improving fluency of calculation for disadvantaged children in Year 3 and Year 4.

After inquiring into the climate, Tim found that colleagues felt under pressure to 'move on' to ensure coverage and wanted more autonomy to slow down and make sure that disadvantaged children understood what was being taught. They also wanted more debate about how best to support disadvantaged children to improve their fluency of calculation.

After inquiring into what was systemic in their teaching of maths across the phase, Tim noticed that teachers often explained calculations to the whole class well enough, but didn't check the understanding of the least advantaged or engage them much in any shared examples.

After inquiring into colleagues' mental models of teaching maths, Tim came to an understanding that, although there was a strong collective agreement on what was involved in a good explanation, teachers were stumped as to how to support the least advantaged children when there were so many gaps in their knowledge. Tim also decided to explore their understanding of maximising children's attention and found that although there was an acceptance that children should concentrate, many of the least advantaged children struggled with this. Tim set a weekly task to read a blog post or extract from a book on topics such as reducing cognitive load, explicitly checking and teaching prerequisite knowledge, the arguments for and against setting, and task design with scaffolding. Meetings would start with a review of what everyone had read and then Tim would encourage the team to commit to trying something different that they had read about.

Building knowledge of colleagues' behaviours

Tim wants to know more about what colleagues are doing differently as a result of their developing knowledge, and so continues to talk to them about what they are trialling and often drops into lessons to see the specific behaviours that colleagues are working on. One teacher has decided to check for understanding with lots of questioning at the guided practice stage, purposefully calling on the disadvantaged children with lower attainment to recall the steps in the process and to suggest what the next step is.

Making a difference

Tim knows that forming habits involves an important reward stage and, after dropping in to see a specific behaviour being trialled, makes sure that he discusses it with colleagues to draw attention to the successes that they notice in how disadvantaged children are responding to colleagues' behaviour change. When he meets with the teacher, he comments on how obvious it is that the disadvantaged children know what is expected of them in their lessons and understand the concept that is being taught. Tim asks what the quality of their work is like as a result of this understanding, and is told that the children work more independently but still occasionally forget steps in a process. Together they discuss ways of making success criteria more permanent and they decide to trial keeping worked examples visible around the room for children to refer back to.

Example scenario: Senior leader

Background

Remember **Madiha**, the headteacher of a large primary school? She is seeking to solve a problem around reading attainment in Key Stage 2, despite children doing well with phonics and decoding.

After inquiring into the climate, Madiha found that there was a mixture of contentment and dissatisfaction with how reading was taught.

After inquiring into teaching practices that were systemic, she noticed that, often, teachers would use resource websites to find stand-alone comprehension activities (a text and some questions) to set a few times a week. Children would simply read the text to themselves and then answer the questions. The only discussion of reading in team meetings was sharing the comprehension sheets that had been chosen.

After inquiring into colleagues' mental models of teaching reading, Madiha ascertained that, in general, the collective understanding of reading included:

- Reading at the end of Key Stage 2 is assessed by reading a text and answering questions, so it makes sense to practise that.
- Parents should be encouraging their children to read more at home.
- Some children with dyslexic tendencies will always find reading difficult.
- Getting better at reading requires lots of practice of skills, such as prediction and inference.

Madiha steered subsequent discussions towards forming a list of the active ingredients for a fledgling reading strategy – concepts and behaviours that need to be present in order to improve the teaching of reading. She also provided examples from other schools on what a sequence of lessons might look like in a reading unit of work, and developed a shared understanding of how a unit would be structured in their school to incorporate those active ingredients. Finally, she wanted to build the team's knowledge of great books by asking them to research and contribute to a reading spine on which they would build units of work. All this knowledge development enabled teams to engage in planning and teaching in a new way.

Building knowledge of colleagues' behaviours

Madiha knows that she needs to focus on how colleagues are applying this knowledge in their planning meetings, because what they create there will influence what will happen in the classroom. She makes sure that other senior leaders are available to join team meetings and contribute to collaborative planning, noticing how the teams bring together a unit of work. In one team, the phase leader starts planning meetings by reminding the team of the active ingredients of the reading strategy, and reinforces the structure of a unit of work that they have agreed by naming and discussing the sequence within each stage.

Making a difference

Madiha knows that habit forming is important and wants to make sure that colleagues' efforts are being rewarded. This will reinforce the behaviour change that she is seeking, so she makes sure that she notices and narrates their efforts to each team, thanking them for their commitment to improving reading. She also knows that to establish this way of working as the norm, she needs to elevate the visibility of what teams are doing (because nobody attends other teams' planning meetings) and amplify approval of their new way of working. To do this, she sets aside time in each weekly meeting for teams to feed back on the units of work that they are planning, where she draws attention to the active ingredients of the reading strategy that are included in the plans. Following this, each team has ten minutes together to discuss any differences in comparison to how they had been planning to decide whether they want to adapt their approach.

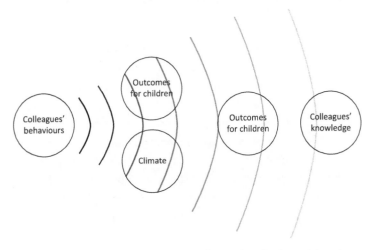

Figure 4.2 *How colleagues' behaviours influence the other impact domains.*

How colleagues plan lessons, teach and manage a class of children directly influences what children learn, and leaders have a significant influence over these behaviours. Colleagues' expectations can be a self-fulfilling prophecy, and helping colleagues to notice and address these is a good use of leaders' time. Colleagues can affect children's motivation by ensuring that they feel successful through skilful scaffolding. A prerequisite to this is their expertise in setting and maintaining social norms, including making sure that children feel a sense of belonging. Leaders can also influence behaviours outside of the classroom that can have an impact on the quality of teaching, such as how colleagues engage with CPD opportunities, as well as those that can have an impact on work–life balance, such as efficiency in the repeated tasks that are required of staff.

5 Outcomes for children

Why outcomes for children matter

Quite simply, schools exist to enable the effective learning of the curriculum. The wide range of wonderful things that leaders pack into their curricula are there either because they have value for their own sake, in order for children to appreciate the beauty of each subject, or because they will have some use in further study or working life. Above all, learning the intended curriculum will give children options at key transition points as they near the end of schooling – options to pursue interests in further study or the world of work, both of which are made easier if children leave each stage of education having learned all that we have intended.

The extent to which children learn our intended curriculum is important, but we also desire an influence beyond the academic, and rightly so. We seek to make a difference to how children behave in order to create a calm and purposeful environment where all feel safe and able to enjoy school life. And of course, we want children to feel happy, safe and that they belong. These conditions are no less important than academic outcomes; indeed, they are a prerequisite for them.

The components of outcomes for children

Statutory assessment places a disproportionate value on some outcomes for children over others, with assessment points dotted across key stages. It is therefore worth considering these outcomes separately from the outcomes of standardised testing and curricular end points.

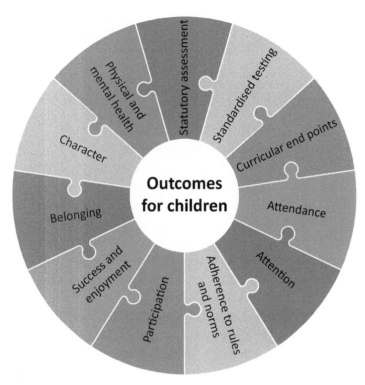

Figure 5.1 *The outcomes for children that leaders might strive for.*

Statutory assessment

Statutory assessment data can be simultaneously too vague and too narrow to be useful. Headline school accountability measures are an aggregate of the attainment of multiple children over years of education. They form the basis of key decisions by parents about where they enrol their children and by multi-academy trusts and local authorities about school support. They can even determine the future of headteachers. Precisely because they are an aggregate and often numerical, they mask the nuance of the information that they represent – namely the school's intended curriculum that children know, understand, remember and can do.

One impact measure that it is important to reject is the flawed logic of expecting improvement from one year to the next in the percentage of children achieving an expected standard. Granted, if this percentage is low and measures of progress are also low, it would suggest that more can be done to improve school performance. However, expecting higher percentages in any given measure *just because* of what they were the previous year fails to recognise the incomparability of the two datasets – different cohorts with different characteristics, opportunities and challenges. Colleagues under dysfunctional line management may be under pressure for children to achieve 'better' than previous cohorts, but such pressure serves to distort the actual work of improvement.

An improvement in progress measures might be considered somewhat more palatable as a measure of impact. The problem is that progress measures are calculated on attainment information, leading to the same risk of curriculum narrowing and gaming, as colleagues divert their attention from what is important to what is measured. Progress measures as an indicator of the impact of school leadership can only seriously be considered over time. It is those responsible for governance, custodians of the school for a period of time, who need to hold themselves to account for supporting colleagues to bring about sustained improvement, not just short-term boom and bust in pursuit of headline numbers. For example, it can be tempting to pile resources into Year 6, as this is where children sit the assessments upon which school effectiveness judgements are made. However, doing so consigns leaders to repeating this pattern each year, whereas investment of resources in the earlier stages of education might prove more beneficial and sustainable in the long term.

Standardised testing

Statutory test scores cannot capture all of what children have learned. In an effort to monitor how well children are doing on their path towards those statutory assessments, and to ascertain whether they have learned what was intended, colleagues may well set internal assessments. Standardised assessment suites give additional indicators of how individual children and cohorts compare against others of the same age nationally. The benefits and drawbacks of standardised testing are discussed later in the chapter.

Curricular outcomes

Curricular outcomes for children should remain rooted in the great context from which they come – the rich curriculum and its specific goals for children to achieve at various points in each subject's sequence. It is the products of a broad and balanced curriculum – not assessment data – that hold beauty. It is the stories that children write, the responses that they give to the books they have read, the mathematical problems that they can solve, the pieces of artwork that they create, the models that they make, the games that they learn to play, the music that they perform and much more that are the real outcomes. These are the things to which we ought to pay attention, narrate and showcase to others, and celebrate.

Curricular outcomes demonstrate what children have achieved, but there are also important milestones to celebrate along the way. Many children will have been set short-term targets – for example as part of SEND support plans – such as:

- reading fluently
- knowing the three times table by heart
- contributing to classroom dialogue.

Each of these examples and many more have an important role to play in achieving longer-term goals, such as those described in the previous paragraph:

- the stories that children write
- the responses that they give to the books they have read

- the mathematical problems that they can solve
- the pieces of artwork that they create
- the models that they make
- the games that they learn to play
- the music that they perform.

These should be the focus of colleagues' attention and should be celebrated. Leaders will see impact in these smaller steps long before final polished pieces of work or improved test scores.

Pastoral outcomes

Pastoral outcomes broadly cover the difference that colleagues make to the behavioural and emotional aspects of school life for children:

- behaviour and attitudes
  - attendance and punctuality
  - attention
  - adhering to rules and norms
  - participation
- personal development
  - success and enjoyment
  - belonging
  - character
  - good physical and mental health.

Behaviour and attitudes

The following aspects of how children behave and the attitudes that sustain them are interconnected and often overlapping, but they all contribute to how it feels for children to come to school.

Attendance and punctuality

It is a fair assumption to make that children who are in school regularly and on time will have a better chance of learning what is intended than if attendance and punctuality are inconsistent.

Attention

Children learn what they pay attention to, so if they learn to better regulate their attention and manage distractions, it is more likely that they will learn the intended curriculum. Colleagues have control over directing children's attention, explained in more detail in Chapter 4.

Adhering to rules and norms

An important element of early child development is the ability to follow direction and to self-regulate when the impulse to follow wants and desires is at odds with a calm and purposeful environment. Schools need rules in order to maintain an environment where children can learn and treat each other respectfully.

Participation

It is reasonable to expect that the more that children participate in classroom and social activities, the more likely it is that they will develop stronger relationships. Participation in talk is vital, whether it is engaging in structured conversations during lessons, asking and answering questions in class or initiating social conversations in the playground.

Personal development

The following outcomes of children's individual and collective behaviour have great importance because they are not only desirable in their own right but can also influence academic outcomes.

Success and enjoyment

The extent to which children experience feelings of success and enjoyment is vital to affirming positive attitudes to learning and forming productive habits. They are parts of a virtuous self-efficacy cycle, where the more that children enjoy something, the more that they will do it, and the more that they do it, the more likely it is that they will get better and experience more success.

Belonging
A feeling of belonging is an important facet of motivation (Walker et al., 2019) and is well worth colleagues aiming to influence. Children feel that they belong when they perceive adults and peers as knowing and caring about them through positive and respectful interactions.

Character
Character can be thought of as correlated concepts of resilience, confidence and independence, all of which are desirable outcomes of teaching.

Good physical and mental health
It is unclear to what extent school conditions contribute to physical and mental health; however, it is worth colleagues paying attention to this area because any positive influence over physical and mental health is desirable.

Should outcomes for children be evaluated?

For each of the different outcomes that leaders might strive for, there are benefits, limitations and trade-offs to consider before deciding whether to evaluate.

Standardised testing

If placing too much emphasis on statutory test results seems short-sighted, with all the resources ploughed into test design, test administration and marking, then placing emphasis on the results gleaned from internally invigilated and marked standardised tests is downright foolhardy. Despite the opportunities for comparability, standardised tests assess only a small sample of the domain studied and, more than likely, assess things that have not necessarily been taught. Moreover, finding a standardised test suite that matches the taught curriculum perfectly is almost impossible.

It is understandable that standardised test scores are valued, because they give the illusion of certainty, but it is important to remember that it is just an illusion. What they can offer is a pointer in the right direction when children *might not* have learned what colleagues expected them to. The useful information is not the numerical information but the learning that the data represents.

We have no control over whether statutory outcomes are measured, but we do have control over measuring outcomes internally. There is a strong tide of common practice when it comes to internally measuring academic outcomes. Standardised tests in reading and maths are popular, but this alone should not be a reason for administering the tests. In making a decision on measuring attainment, we should consider the benefits and limitations of standardised testing, which can be seen in Table 5.1.

Table 5.1 The benefits and limitations of standardised testing for measuring attainment.

Benefits	Limitations
They allow for an external reference for children's attainment compared to national averages.	They are very unlikely to be aligned with the school curriculum.
They allow for the comparison of performance of groups of children and cohorts.	A change in score does not necessarily mean that a child has or has not made progress.
They allow for the reporting of somewhat meaningful trends to those in charge of governance.	There is no standardisation of test administration between schools.
	Tests are not necessarily a good indicator of a child's understanding – they are a one-off performance.
	Standardised score calibration from publishers may be dated.

Teacher assessments

Another option for measuring outcomes is to collect teacher assessments in subjects. Most schools that measure attainment in this way have some sort of grading system, usually similar to how attainment is reported to the DfE at the end of Key Stage 1 and 2, classifying children as having 'met the expected standard', 'working towards the expected standard' and having 'exceeded the expected standard'. Once again, being common practice is not the right reason to measure outcomes in this way. It is useful to consider the benefits and limitations, a summary of which can be seen in Table 5.2.

Table 5.2 The benefits and limitations of teacher assessment for measuring attainment.

Benefits	Limitations
Teacher assessments might be able to provide an indicator of the extent to which groups or cohorts are keeping up with the curriculum.	Teacher assessments are unavoidably biased because teachers are human. The boundaries between grades are vague; what constitutes the expected standard? What does it take to have exceeded it? Does exceeding mean having learned more than what was taught? At what point does a child move from working towards it to meeting it? Moderation can be time-consuming.

A trade-off

The benefits of both standardised testing and teacher assessment do not, however, consider the trade-off that comes with them – the workload associated with administering, marking and moderating assessments, as well as inputting data into a tracking system and analysing that data. Despite a reduction in hours worked on administrative tasks (which includes assessment practices) from 2016 to 2019, teachers continue to report spending too much time on such work (Mccrea, 2020). We must be sure that the benefits of any form of assessment are worth colleagues' time and, if so, seek ways in which to minimise the workload associated with it. For example, we might choose online assessments that are marked automatically rather than paper copies that require colleagues to mark them. We might also choose to have fewer data-collection points throughout the year for teacher assessment.

Formative assessment

It is not the evaluation of outcomes for children that is important; what is important is colleagues building knowledge of what children do and don't understand in order to make adjustments to teaching. This is by far the most useful activity for colleagues, and the tension for leaders to resolve is to free up time for this. We cannot avoid the need for the evaluation of children's learning at scale for accountability purposes, but we can make sure that we protect colleagues' time and attention, enabling them to focus on what actually makes a difference to children's learning.

Pastoral outcomes

Pastoral outcomes are well worth colleagues' attention, even if they make little or no difference to academic outcomes. Pastoral outcomes address broader motivations for schooling than simply learning the curriculum, and are often part of a school's wider mission. Inquiring into pastoral outcomes can help leaders to understand more fully the nature of the specific problem that is being tackled – and this knowledge can be vital in directing colleagues' attention to what children need in order to flourish.

Building knowledge of outcomes for children

There has always been an emphasis on assessing the core subjects because of the requirements of statutory assessment, but doing so risks narrowing the curriculum through either the explicit or the implicit communication about their importance over other subjects. If we value curriculum and subject content well enough to teach it, then surely it is worth trying to find out whether children have actually learned it.

Standardised testing

If we decide to try to measure attainment with standardised tests (remembering that, although they are based on the National Curriculum, they probably do not align with what we've taught), there are some choices about which measures can be used to support evaluation. Most suites offer a range of information, such as:

- standardised scores that give an average range against which to compare individual performance
- an attainment age that can be compared to chronological age
- scaled scores
- percentile rank.

None of these measures are useful for individual teachers because they do not draw attention to what children have or have not understood. This data is fit only for those responsible for governance, and possibly for parents (along with a health warning and a clear understanding of what they actually mean).

Teacher assessment

Choosing a teacher assessment system that captures what teachers think children have learned is fraught with difficulty. Because learning is invisible, teachers can only base judgements on proxies, such as the work that children produce. Then there is the issue of the validity of using classwork (which is unlikely to be independent) to make judgements on what has been learned. Further, there is so much curriculum content that assessing it all would be impossible. Leaders have to accept these conditions and make decisions based on the inevitable unreliability of the information gathered. If we are going to make broad assessments of an entire domain such as maths, reading or writing:

- Don't pretend that teachers can make accurate assessments; instead, encourage quick judgements based on hunches to remove unnecessary workload.

- Use a simple binary grading system that categorises children as having learned or not learned what was intended (with the caveat of understanding the difference between learning and performance).

This second point fits better with a system that deliberately seeks to capture what children have learned about the specific, highest-value parts of the curriculum. The phonics screening check in Year 1 does not claim to assess the whole domain of reading – just phonetic awareness and decoding at a crucial stage of development. The multiplication tables check in Year 4 does not claim to assess the whole domain in maths – just speed of recall for some of the trickiest times tables at a crucial stage of development. Perhaps our internal assessments need to follow suit to provide information for colleagues that is more useful and more reliable.

Whichever measure is chosen, leaders need to remember that measurement demands evaluation. A child's score on one test is not necessarily indicative of what that child has learned. Just because group and cohort data is a combination of individual data, it doesn't make it more accurate or reliable. The percentage of children at whatever the expected standard is, or an average standardised score, is still indicative rather than absolute, hiding away all the useful contextual information.

How often assessments are carried out

Leaders have decisions to make about how often assessments are carried out and why. Sometimes leaders make such decisions influenced by aspects of school life, rather than what it is they want to find out. Just because there are six half-terms in a year, it does not mean that there should be six rounds of assessment. When assessments are administered is an important consideration. For example, if they are set at the end of term, children might not perform to their potential because they (and colleagues) might be tired. Carrying out an assessment at the end of a term seems to imply that the aim is to measure what has been learned that term. This is misguided when it comes to standardised tests, as they almost certainly do not assess a school's implemented curriculum. If they are school-devised assessments, setting them at the end of term is a timing that is not based on logic. Learning does not click for children at a given point in time. Any assessment seeks to check what children have learned up to that point; there is no more reason to do them in the last week of a term than any other.

The status of assessment

Then there is the importance that leaders deliberately or unconsciously assign to tests. If leaders choose to administer standardised tests, then they ought to take reliability into consideration in terms of how they are invigilated. National data provided by publishers is based on standardised invigilation, and if we're to make more valid inferences, then we need to create the same testing conditions. However, doing so might raise the perceived stakes of these assessments in the eyes of both teachers and children, which can be compounded with how leaders use the data that results. Leaders should do everything possible to downplay the stakes, to avoid gaming or diversion of effort to teach to the test. Because standardised tests draw results from multiple schools, how other leaders in other schools administer the tests will impact the outcomes, which of course is out of anyone's control.

Building knowledge of curricular outcomes

To build knowledge of curriculur outcomes for children that does not rely on tests, leaders might look at how pieces of work compare to the standard expected or modelled by colleagues. Careful analysis of every curricular outcome for every child is not possible, though, so perhaps it would be more useful for leaders to sample the work produced by children at particular points in a curriculum's sequence.

Arguably, the real measure of how good a school is can be found in the work that the least advantaged children produce. Children from advantaged backgrounds are far more likely to flourish regardless of what happens in the classroom, but for many disadvantaged children, if they are not getting the right support in the classroom, they might not be getting any support at all. Therefore, one could argue that it is the work that the least advantaged children produce that leaders really need to inquire into.

Workbook scrutiny is already a common practice, but the devil is in the detail of how it is carried out. The work that children produce is probably not a reliable indicator of what they have learned, but it does indicate what colleagues and children have been paying attention to. It suggests the standard that colleagues expect from children and that children have for themselves. And of course it is not just the outcomes of a sequence of learning that are useful to inquire into. These outcomes are dependent on the careful sequencing of smaller chunks of learning, and it could be a worthwhile exercise for leaders to build their knowledge of how children are doing in the earlier stages of a unit of work through looking at and discussing with children and teachers what is recorded in books.

Then there is the consideration of how leaders go about looking at the work in children's books. What is important is discussion – what children say about the work that they have produced. This will yield far more interesting information than looking at books without the children or, indeed, the colleagues who have taught those lessons. Leaders can gain a better insight through hearing from colleagues and children about the work produced.

Building knowledge of pastoral outcomes

Children's behavioural habits are commonly visible in day-to-day school activities and interactions, but they may not be the most useful indicators of pastoral outcomes for children. Some of these outcomes, such as how children feel about school, their confidence, the feeling of safety, etc., exist only in the minds of children, and although their actions can imply what they believe, value and how they are feeling, it can be more valuable to seek out their beliefs about school life, their social experiences and their emotional states in order to find out what drives the observable behaviour.

Teachers' observations of children and discussions with them during everyday activities can yield plenty of useful information. Introducing a means of measurement, as discussed below, might add value by revealing the aspects of children's lives not visible to colleagues – there will be countless interactions that go unobserved and opinions that go unsaid.

Observations of children

Children's behaviours can be quantified through tallying the occurrence of target behaviours, such as initiating conversations with peers on the playground, counting the number of interruptions they cause or tracking the time spent on-task during lessons, for example. Qualitative information could also be gathered, such as what they say to their talking partner when prompted to talk or what they say about the work that they have undertaken.

Discussions with children

Leaders' knowledge can be built through conversation. Simple questions could become part of planned child–adult interactions, such as:

- In which lesson did you work hardest today? Why do you think that is?
- In which lesson did you do your best work today? What was good about it?
- What did you do when you found work hard today?
- Whom did you play with at break time? What did you play? How did it make you feel?
- What emotions have you felt today? What did you do to feel better?

Surveys

While observations and discussions can provide colleagues with useful information about individual children, some form of measurement might be required to look at trends across groups, cohorts and the whole school. Children's perceptions could be gathered at scale through surveys. When carrying out a survey, the age and stage of development of the children need to be taken into account – for example, if children cannot read and respond, they could listen and respond. In addition, when tackling specific problems, it is far more useful to survey children about specific issues rather than to carry out a generic annual survey.

What could we do with the knowledge that we've built about outcomes for children?

Any information gathered must be used in order for the time spent on gathering it to be worthwhile. This is another reason why it is more useful to build knowledge of a specific problem rather than to collect data and then decide what to do with it.

A starting point for further inquiry

When evaluating assessment data, it is important to challenge the illusion of certainty. Any numerical data that comes from statutory assessments is stripped of context and is only a starting point for further inquiry. If leaders are to analyse one cohort's data, it should be done alongside any relevant contextual information. Comparing cohorts lacks validity, and so leaders need to ask: What is the trend over time that these results contribute to? Regardless of what is measured or how, what matters is what leaders do with the information.

Any measure of what children have learned can only be an indicator of their actual understanding. Whether it is a standardised test score or a teacher assessment, the sensible thing to do is to treat the data as a starting point to find out the information that might actually be useful for colleagues: what children understand and what they don't, the misconceptions that children might have and the barriers that they face to keeping up with the demands of the curriculum, such as patchy prior knowledge, poor attendance or special educational needs. Assessment can be a valuable exercise if colleagues settle on actions to address the reasons for children not learning what was intended.

Acting on the knowledge built

Ensuring that action is based on the knowledge built about outcomes for children can be supported by applying a useful rubric.

The curriculum

Are the sequences of lessons or units of work conducive to children building understanding?

Is there time built in to check and, if necessary, teach prerequisites to the upcoming content?

Do certain topics or concepts need to come back around for review?

Pedagogy

Do teachers need to focus on encouraging children to put more effort in?

Are teachers explaining concepts clearly?

Are scaffolds fit for purpose and removed gradually?

Is there a need for more guided practice in lessons?

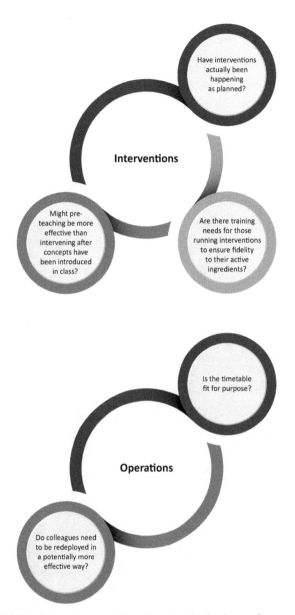

Figure 5.2 *Possible actions to take based on what leaders know of outcomes for children.*

Leaders might consider improvements that could be made to the areas shown in Figure 5.2.

Celebrating success

Having evaluated the quality of children's work, celebrating success is a useful form of standardisation. Showing children and colleagues examples of great work that children are capable of can recalibrate what they think possible and hopefully result in an increase in standards the next time that unit of work is taught. It can also help to tailor the next unit of work that children study if misconceptions are picked up. Finally, the unit of work itself can be adapted so that the next cohort of children that study it have an improved experience in comparison to the last.

Example scenario: Middle leader

Background

Remember **Tim**, a lower Key Stage 2 phase leader in a two-form-entry primary school? He has a particular problem to solve around improving fluency of calculation for disadvantaged children in Year 3 and Year 4.

After inquiring into the climate, Tim found that colleagues felt under pressure to 'move on' to ensure coverage and wanted more autonomy to slow down and make sure that disadvantaged children understood what was being taught. They also wanted more debate about how best to support disadvantaged children to improve their fluency of calculation.

After inquiring into what was systemic in their teaching of maths across the phase, Tim noticed that teachers often explained concepts to the whole class well enough, but didn't check the understanding of the least advantaged or engage them much in any shared examples, instead taking the responses from a few children as an indicator that it was time to move on.

After inquiring into colleagues' mental models of teaching maths, Tim came to an understanding that, although there was a strong collective agreement on what was involved in a good explanation, teachers were stumped as to how to support the least advantaged children when there were so many gaps in their knowledge. Tim also decided to explore the team's understanding of maximising children's attention, and found that although there was an acceptance that children should concentrate, many of the least advantaged children struggled with this. Tim set a weekly task to read a blog post or extract from a book on topics such as reducing cognitive load, explicitly checking and teaching prerequisite knowledge, the arguments for and against setting, and task design with scaffolding. Meetings would start with a review of what everyone had read and then Tim would encourage the team to commit to trying something different based on what they had read.

After inquiring into colleagues' behaviours, Tim found that one teacher in particular started asking more questions during guided practice to check the understanding of the least advantaged children.

Building knowledge of outcomes for children

Tim now needs to find out the difference that this is making to the children. He knows that just because children seem to understand in the lesson, this does not mean that they have learned anything – although understanding is certainly desirable. Therefore, when he watches what children are doing in his colleague's lesson, he simply wants to know whether the least advantaged children are engaging with the teacher's modelling and how well they can get on with the work that is set. It appears that the children do indeed respond with understanding to the teacher's questions and, with support, keep on task and experience some success. Careful not to declare victory too soon, Tim also wants to know whether they will still understand the next day, the next week and the next month. In order to ascertain this, Tim knows that watching lessons isn't necessarily the most effective approach. To see how much children have retained, a better approach is simply to talk to the children about the work that they have produced to see the extent to which they can talk confidently about what they have learned. Tim even includes a few related questions to see how they will respond. Although most children find this difficult, Tim is hopeful. A few prompts and the children seem to remember more and grow in confidence.

Making a difference

The conversations that Tim has with the children about what they have remembered from previous lessons have a number of benefits. They demonstrate to the children that teachers care about their learning, and they give those children who are spoken to another interaction with lesson content to strengthen their mental model of the concept. They also provide Tim and his colleague with a point of discussion in order for Tim to reinforce the purpose that has been established of paying attention to the mathematical achievements of the least advantaged children. By sharing the children's successes, Tim is contributing to a positive climate in the team and, by raising it in team meetings, strengthening the system of thinking about and making arrangements for the least advantaged.

Background

Remember **Madiha**, the headteacher of a large primary school? She has a particular problem to solve in relation to improving reading attainment in Key Stage 2, despite children doing well with phonics and decoding.

After inquiring into the climate, Madiha found that there was a mixture of contentment and dissatisfaction with how reading was taught.

After inquiring into teaching practices that were systemic, she noticed that, often, teachers would use resources websites to find stand-alone comprehension activities (a text and some questions) to set a few times a week. Children would simply read the text to themselves and then answer the questions. The only discussion of reading in team meetings was sharing the comprehension sheets that had been chosen.

After inquiring into colleagues' mental models of teaching reading, Madiha ascertained that, in general, the collective understanding of reading included:

- Reading at the end of Key Stage 2 is assessed by reading a text and answering questions, so it makes sense to practise that.
- Parents should be encouraging their children to read more at home.
- Some children with dyslexic tendencies will always find reading difficult.
- Getting better at reading requires lots of practice of skills, such as prediction and inference.

Outcomes for children

Madiha steered subsequent discussions towards forming a list of the active ingredients for a fledgling reading strategy – concepts and behaviours that need to be present in order to improve the teaching of reading. She also provided examples from other schools on what a sequence of lessons might look like in a reading unit of work, and developed a shared understanding of how a unit would be structured in their school to incorporate those active ingredients. Finally, she wanted to build the team's knowledge of great books by asking them to research and contribute to a reading spine on which to build units of work. All this knowledge development enabled teams to engage in planning and teaching in a new way.

After inquiring into colleagues' behaviours, Madiha noticed that, in one team in particular, meetings included a lot of discussion and reinforcement of the active ingredients of the reading strategy.

Building knowledge of outcomes for children

Madiha now needs to find out the extent to which the changes in colleagues' behaviour are influencing outcomes for children. She ascertains that the best way to do this is to have conversations with children about the texts that they have been studying. She prepares by checking on the vocabulary that the children have been taught and the background knowledge that colleagues have chosen to explicitly teach to support children's comprehension. In these conversations with children, she asks open questions about the text, such as:

- Tell me about what you liked.
- Tell me about what you disliked.
- Tell me about what puzzled you.

- Tell me about any patterns that you noticed.
- Tell me about the most interesting character.

In some instances, children talk using the vocabulary that they have been taught, and their responses demonstrate that they also have an understanding of the background knowledge that has been taught in lessons. When this is not the case, Madiha prompts them more specifically with questions such as asking the meaning of specific words and what general knowledge they need to know to understand the text. With these direct questions, children are better at talking about the text. She also listens to some children reading, asking them to do so with expression. Madiha is pleased with how many children are able to achieve this.

Making a difference

These interactions with the children give Madiha a chance to reinforce the difference that they are making in the various impact domains. Children are pleased to talk confidently about what they are learning, which plays a part in reinforcing their efforts in class. It keeps momentum going with children around the idea that the school thinks reading is important. The children that Madiha speaks to have additional interactions with the text that can deepen their understanding. Madiha also has much to talk to colleagues about from these conversations, enabling her to keep the team focused on reading. She enjoys sharing the success of the children and knows that doing so will contribute to the increasingly positive climate around reading. These conversations also serve to reinforce the systems that are being established in team meetings, as she narrates the whole process to other phase leaders and colleagues.

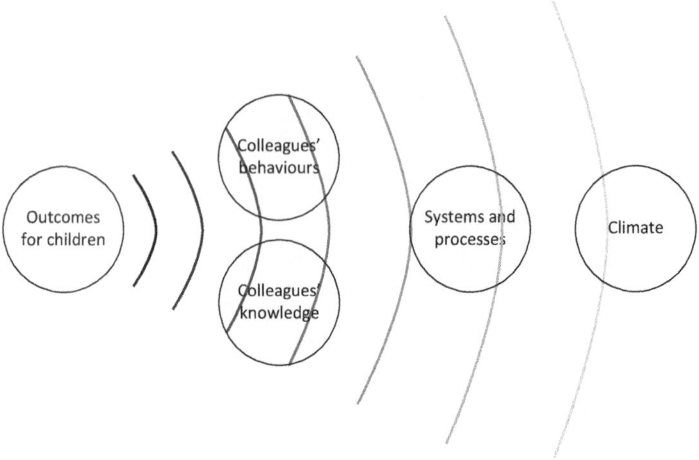

Figure 5.3 *How outcomes for children influence the other impact domains.*

School improvement is ultimately about improving outcomes for children, but there is more to those outcomes than attainment and progress in statutory tests. The curricular end points that children produce or perform are the true outcomes of a well-designed curriculum. When outcomes are reduced to assessment data, this gives the illusion of certainty, but assessments can only cover small samples of the entire domain of what has been taught and can often be unreliable measures of what children have actually learned. If leaders choose to measure attainment, the data should only be a starting point for building knowledge of outcomes for children – what matters is what leaders do with the information that they gather.

A calm and purposeful atmosphere is the result of the collective behaviour and attitudes of children and enables the ultimate goal of children learning the intended curriculum. It is children's beliefs and attitudes that sustain how they behave and treat each other, contributing to how it feels to come to school for all children. Inquiring into pastoral outcomes for children can be achieved on an individual basis through observing and talking to them or, at scale, through surveys, which can identify trends. Leaders can use the knowledge that they have built of pastoral outcomes for children to bring about improvement to how it feels for children to come to school.

Using the five-part framework to make a difference

6 A theory of change

School leadership improves teaching and learning, indirectly and most powerfully, by improving the status of significant key classroom and school conditions.

Leithwood, Harris and Hopkins (2019, p. 6)

What is a theory of change?

A theory of change is a way of supporting leaders to have an impact. While Section 1 explores the impact domains, this chapter describes how leaders might use the framework to make a difference. This theory of change makes several assumptions:

1. A simple cause and effect relationship between domains does not exist.

2. The impact domains are interrelated, each influencing the others in ways that we might predict *and* ways that we cannot predict.

3. Each impact domain (and its components described in Section 1) is in a constant state of change.

4. *I* and *we* are two sides of the same coin: actions of individual colleagues can affect a team, and the actions of a team can affect individual colleagues.

5. Leaders affect outcomes for children indirectly; it is the interactions at staff level and between colleagues and children that make a difference.

6. Improvement initiatives are never completely successful; some children and colleagues will be advantaged by what we do, while others will be disadvantaged.

What this model is not

We are hardwired to look for patterns – to make sense of the world. It is tempting to expect and plot a course towards better outcomes for children that is linear. For example:

- If children are to succeed, we need motivated colleagues who are committed to the children, to the school and to the profession.
- If colleagues are to feel committed, we need good systems for curriculum planning, teaching, assessment, behaviour and CPD.
- If these systems are to take hold, individual colleagues need to do new things or do existing things better.
- If individual colleagues are to improve their practice, they need to know more.

How each domain influences the others

The linear, cause and effect conception of impact described above is probably not the reality of making a difference in schools. While it is true that leaders *can* have an impact on these domains *in this order*, our actions, the actions of colleagues and the actions of children have their own unforeseen and unintended consequences, each affecting the other domains.

The influence of colleagues' knowledge

If colleagues know more about their subject, about effective pedagogy, and about strategies for improvement and leaders' reasoning behind them, they are in a position to modify their behaviours. Arguably, adopting new behaviours or refining existing ones cannot be done without first knowing more about those behaviours. Mimicry of desirable behaviours without understanding is a likely result of leaders' inattention to colleagues' knowledge.

What colleagues know influences how they feel, which contributes to climate. The information that leaders share (or don't share) with colleagues affects their feeling of psychological safety, trust, purpose or shared confidence in the team.

While it is easy to conceive how colleagues' knowledge might influence what they do and how they feel at work, it is perhaps harder to see how it influences systems and processes. But it probably does. Every school will have all sorts of systems for planning, teaching, behaviour and CPD. If those systems are to be effective, colleagues need to *know* what they consist of, how they work and why they are there. Their hidden knowledge of the school's systems likely has an indirect influence over the quality of those systems – the extent to which they are consistent and contributing to the other impact domains.

Then there is the influence of knowledge on outcomes for children. Great teaching involves knowing what children do or do not understand, what they can and cannot do. It involves knowing what makes children tick, what motivates them and sometimes how to cajole them into concentrating more or working harder. The link between what colleagues know and outcomes for children is the actions that we take. Clearly, such actions cannot be taken without that hidden knowledge of children – that knowledge enables the action that we take.

The influence of colleagues' behaviours

What colleagues do, day in, day out, probably has the most easily recognisable impact on each of the other domains. In pursuit of the ultimate impact of better outcomes for children, colleagues' behaviours influence what children learn – not just academically, but socially too. It is the strength of this connection that leaders must seek to understand. When a teacher explains something beautifully or piques a child's interest, the child might go away and pursue that interest, learning more than the teacher had intended. We would like to think that this is straightforward cause and effect, but there are other elements at play because the likelihood is that not all children would have done the same. It could be possible, for example, that an enabling parent inquired into what the child had done that day and provided support to explore further.

We also have to consider that the connection between what colleagues do and what children learn can be very weak. Children might learn *despite* our attempts. A teacher might have explained short division poorly and set tasks that did not result in the child understanding the concept at the time. That same child may well have a parent, sibling or tutor who remedies this misunderstanding. This would be unknowable to the teacher; in this instance, all that is known is that the teacher taught short division and the child learned short division.

Colleagues' habits also contribute to what *they* come to know. Building formal knowledge relevant to education requires behaviours such as engagement with CPD. The habit of conversation is another important behaviour by which colleagues might build their hidden knowledge of each other and of school-specific strategies and systems. Colleagues' behaviour also contributes to what other staff know. For example, the efforts of leaders to design and provide CPD have the aim of building colleagues' knowledge and, ideally, a collective understanding of, for example, what makes great teaching. The act of teaching itself contributes to colleagues' hidden knowledge of strategies that will have appeared to be successful (or not) in the classroom.

How colleagues behave influences the climate. The interactions between colleagues provide the moments where psychological safety is developed (or damaged) and where trust is built (or lost). This applies to all colleagues and not just leaders. Leaders might set the tone for a positive climate with their actions but, for many colleagues, leaders are not the people with whom they interact most each day. Colleagues need those more regular interactions with whomever they work with closely to be conducive to a positive climate. We may all work in the same school but colleagues experience climate in different ways, depending on with whom they spend their time and how others behave towards and around them.

What colleagues do influences the systems that become established or reinforced. Leaders might influence enough colleagues to, for example, use concrete manipulatives to teach maths. Colleagues talk about their use, children come to expect their presence in the classroom and it therefore becomes systemic. However, this can also work in a negative way. If a critical mass of colleagues do not, for example, address low-level disruption, turning a blind eye to it, then it is possible for groups of children and teachers to come to an unspoken understanding that the children won't cause disruption and the teachers won't push them to work hard.

The majority of colleagues acting in a particular way as a result of leaders' actions is one possible way in which behaviours can affect systems, but the influence might come from anywhere – not just from leaders. There will also be influential colleagues around the school whom others look up to and imitate, which is entirely unplanned by leaders. Behaviour change can ripple around a school – for example, one colleague might have read about a way of scaffolding to support children with writing and tried it with success in their class. They might have chatted to someone else in the staffroom about it, which resulted in that colleague coming to see it in action and having a go themselves. If this happens a few more times with different people and enough success is attributed to the strategy in question, it is easy to see how it might become systemic without leaders' design.

The influence of systems and processes

Systems and processes are the way in which the school runs – the collective actions of the team. These systems influence the climate because they include the things that make a difference to it, such as workload, how behaviour is managed and the professional development on offer.

A school's systems influence what individual colleagues do. They determine the ways in which colleagues interact with each other and with children. They determine how colleagues spend their working time and the extent to which they develop and refine their practice. And they also determine the extent to which colleagues feel motivated and part of a team and the extent to which they have autonomy over what they do.

Systems influence what colleagues know. They guide colleagues towards what to think about, focusing their attention on agreed priorities. The best example of this is a school's system for professional development, but there are many other systems that also influence colleagues' knowledge. A behaviour system that prioritises the building of positive relationships will guide colleagues to engage with it more, whether through conversation or through personal research.

The way in which the curriculum is mapped out will influence colleagues to look further into the elements of that system. For example, if key concepts are highlighted and threaded through the curriculum, such as the concept of 'empire' in history, this focuses attention on the concept and will probably influence what colleagues come to know about it. In turn, teachers can ascertain children's understanding of the concept by introducing a pedagogical system of regular quizzing. With more opportunities to reveal what children are thinking, colleagues can quite easily pick up more about what has been understood than they otherwise might.

Systems influence outcomes for children. Well-run behaviour systems could make children feel safe and result in better concentration in lessons. A carefully designed curriculum, taught well, can certainly affect what children think about and, in turn, learn.

The influence of climate

As discussed, climate is the collective feeling of motivation, psychological safety, the experience of autonomy, high levels of trust between colleagues, and a shared, clear purpose. If colleagues are feeling all of those things, it is likely to influence how they behave. This might take the form of more engagement in professional development, in better-quality conversations with colleagues, or in more relaxed, warm interactions with children.

Climate influences what colleagues know. With more autonomy, for example, colleagues can develop aspects of subject or pedagogical knowledge that they might not otherwise have come across using the established professional development systems in school. A climate of trust and psychological safety might also lead to colleagues having a more developed hidden knowledge of each other, knowing what makes each other tick and the kind of feedback and challenge that everyone finds most useful.

Climate has an impact on how colleagues behave. Those experiencing psychological safety and trust are more likely to take professional risks, such as trying out new ideas in the classroom, free from fear of reprisal.

The influence of outcomes for children

Outcomes for children influence what colleagues do. In one lesson alone, colleagues will receive a huge amount of feedback based on the responses that children provide – the essence of responsive teaching. Those same outcomes for children also influence what colleagues know because, of course, we would not be able to take responsive action without understanding in the first place.

Outcomes for children influence the climate. The feeling of success that we experience when children succeed is one of the great joys of teaching. It can contribute to a feeling of flow.

Outcomes for children influence systems and processes. A system designed to reduce low-level disruption, for example, could well be incredibly successful. A reduction in minor disruption is certainly a desirable outcome for children, but would render the original system unnecessary. That system would probably then evolve because the needs of the children will have changed.

The complexity of schools

Schools are far from simple organisations due to the innumerable, unpredictable interactions between colleagues and children that take place each day, but neither can they be described as complicated. A complicated system can be fully understood because of the predictable relationships between cause and effect. Complexity is not the same as complication. What makes a system complex is the interconnected domains that make prediction of cause and effect almost impossible. Individual classrooms and entire schools are perfect examples of this.

It is not uncommon for a phase or school to evade improvement efforts. When we conceive of actions and carry them out, it is possible for them not to work out as we had planned. For example, we may completely misjudge timeframes, we might think that we were clear in what we wanted when it turns out that we weren't, and we might even make things worse, despite noble intentions.

Accepting the complex nature of schools can be reassuring for leaders, providing an explanation as to why previous initiatives might not have worked out as desired. But it can also cause a feeling of hopelessness – that we're not in control as much as we like to think that we are.

In even the smallest of teams or schools, there will be many interactions between colleagues, the consequences of which cannot be predicted. It is in these unpredictable exchanges that innovation arises. To make a difference, leaders must pay attention to what is happening between colleagues – what they are talking about and how they are communicating. It is these interactions where improvement resides.

Impact – where to start

It can be daunting to choose where to start when realising the complexity of school life. Essentially, leaders need to choose the right problem and then dig a little deeper to have the best chance of selecting from the possible solutions.

Choosing the right problem

Leaders need to understand the difference between change and improvement. The former might include leaders 'putting their mark' on a team or a school – superficial change such as the school logo, the uniform, when the team routinely meets or adopting the marking policy developed in a previous school. But change can have an unnecessary negative effect on climate, colleagues' behaviours and perhaps even outcomes for children.

Improvement requires leaders to identify the right problem to which to pay attention – the more specific, the better. 'Low maths attainment' or 'low-level disruption' are too broad because these examples are undoubtedly localised in certain classrooms, year groups or subjects and are not by any means universal. Despite this, they may be a good starting point for focusing our attention on a specific problem.

Digging deeper

Just as Tim and Madiha did in Section 1, leaders need to explore a problem in great depth in order to be able to select appropriate solutions and bring about improvement, rather than simply change. This is where the impact framework is helpful because it provides different lenses through which to examine a problem. If leaders identified low-level disruption as a broad problem that needs further exploration, they could seek to understand, for example:

- what colleagues know about:
  - the behaviours that are disruptive
  - the behaviour policy

- possible strategies for addressing low-level disruption
- what makes great teaching
- what colleagues do:
  - to pre-empt disruptive behaviour
  - when addressing disruptive behaviour
- the systems and processes for:
  - what happens when rules are broken
  - how children are expected to work
  - children moving around the school
- the climate in terms of:
  - autonomy over managing behaviour
  - the sense of shared purpose for managing behaviour
  - the extent to which colleagues feel successful
  - indicators of psychological safety and trust among the team
- outcomes for children in terms of:
  - when disruptive behaviour happens and when it does not
  - the extent to which children feel safe
  - the established norms for how children behave
  - children's understanding of what is expected of them.

Watching and listening will help us to understand more about school life in the impact domains. This isn't about lesson observations (mainly in this case because by being in lessons we probably influence what is happening and will not see the reality of what normally happens); it is about conversations – inquiring into colleagues' understanding and experiences and building knowledge through what we might notice on walks of the phase or the school. These conversations can start to have an immediate impact on climate simply through us paying attention to and showing that we care about an issue that might be blighting colleagues' day-to-day experiences. Building knowledge is an important and necessary step in the right direction.

Choosing solutions

The process of building knowledge puts us in a far better position to choose what to do because, hopefully, it will have revealed the specifics of the problem. It is also a way of preventing us from just transplanting others' solutions, either from our previous schools or from what other schools are currently doing. Using others' solutions to their problems in our school is probably not going to effectively tackle our problem because it will have manifested differently. Nothing works everywhere.

Putting colleagues first

The more direct influencers of outcomes for children are teaching colleagues, not leaders. This theory of change recognises that although the ultimate desired impact is improved outcomes for children, colleagues need to flourish before children can. *Putting children first* is a common sentiment but only serves to skew leaders' thinking. It is difficult to challenge because it sounds so virtuous and appeals to our instinct to protect. Even so, the mantra is flawed. What leaders should be doing is not putting children first but acting to realise the ultimate aim of improving outcomes for children. The difference between the words *first* and *ultimate* is significant. They are near antonyms, and this exemplifies an important point when it comes to making a difference in schools: that the ends do not necessarily resemble the means. It is the quality of teaching that is the biggest factor that can make a difference to achievement (Coe et al., 2014), and colleagues who are flourishing are more likely to sustain the high performance that is necessary in order for children to succeed.

Leaders have most influence over what colleagues know

Improvement in behaviours, systems and processes, climate or outcomes for children is unlikely without colleagues knowing more about the specific problem that we are trying to solve or having better connected mental models of great teaching.

One option for leaders to develop what colleagues know is through the big launch of an initiative: all colleagues together with the aim of developing a collective understanding of what everyone will be doing to tackle a specific problem. What will likely happen is that, as leaders, we will perceive the message that we send to be clear, probably because we will have spent more time than other colleagues thinking about it than they will have. However, we have to accept that there will be lots of misunderstanding and lots of misinterpretation that require many, many interactions before we can come to a genuine shared understanding. Improvement happens through these multiple interactions – daily conversations about the problem, what we are doing to address it and how those efforts are going.

Beyond building knowledge

The impact domains of colleagues' behaviours, systems and processes, climate and outcomes for children all interact in ways that we might sometimes be able to predict, but in many ways that we cannot. As such, there is no defined sequence through the impact domains.

> *Taking complexity seriously is an invitation to pay attention differently.*
> Chris Mowles (2021, p. 175)

Paying attention differently is to reject simple cause-and-effect relationships between actions and outcomes. It is to appreciate the connections between each impact domain, using the framework to focus our attention on all the things that might make a difference to what we are ultimately striving for – better outcomes for children.

7 Exemplars of using the impact framework

This chapter provides five examples of the impact that leaders might seek when addressing common, specific problems:

- **Example 1:** Improving reading attainment in Year 2/Year 3 children who were on the cusp of the expected standard in the phonics screening check
- **Example 2:** Improving maths attainment in lower Key Stage 2 for children not yet fluent in recall of number facts/calculations
- **Example 3:** Improving behaviour during break and lunch in upper Key Stage 2
- **Example 4:** Improving provision for children with SEND/who are disadvantaged in writing
- **Example 5:** Improving the coherence and the sequencing of the history curriculum

Each example provides an idea of the impact that leaders might need to seek in each domain in order to effectively address the problem, providing leaders with a suggestion of the kinds of areas that might need paying attention to.

These examples can be useful for leaders in the many day-to-day school situations where we are required to think about the impact that we have made or are aiming to make, including:

- strategic, whole-school improvement planning
- improvement planning for certain aspects of school life, such as a middle leader's action plan
- explaining progress towards Ofsted areas for improvement
- responding to challenges from those responsible for governance
- throughout the appraisal cycle.

Example 1: Improving reading attainment in Year 2/Year 3 children who were on the cusp of the expected standard in the phonics screening check

Colleagues' knowledge	Colleagues' behaviour	Systems and processes	Climate	Outcomes for children
Colleagues know more about how children learn to read (simple view of reading; phonics/fluency/prosody/language acquisition).	Colleagues have higher expectations of all in terms of their effort and what they are capable of with reading, particularly those disadvantaged in some way (paying attention, quality feedback).	Leaders provide regular and iterative CPD opportunities for colleagues to get better at teaching reading, including collaborative planning.	Colleagues feel that they have autonomy over how they teach reading.	Children achieve well in statutory tests (phonics check/Key Stage 1 SATs/Key Stage 2 SATs).

Colleagues' knowledge	Colleagues' behaviour	Systems and processes	Climate	Outcomes for children
Colleagues understand the chosen phonics programme (including common misconceptions) and the school's reading strategy.	Colleagues model and explain fluent reading clearly, presenting new ideas in small steps and with scaffolding.	Leaders present a clear school strategy for the teaching of reading, including active ingredients understood by all.	Colleagues experience flow when planning and teaching reading (clear goals, just the right difficulty and deeply satisfying).	Children achieve well in internal assessments (phonics/fluency, standardised tests).
Colleagues understand the active ingredients of the reading strategy and know more about how to teach phonics/fluency/prosody/language acquisition.	Colleagues are better at responsive teaching – checking understanding and addressing misconceptions.	There is a coherent, well-sequenced reading curriculum that is well resourced.	Colleagues have a clear purpose for the teaching of reading.	Children with SEND support plans meet relevant short-term targets for reading.

Impact

Colleagues' knowledge	Colleagues' behaviour	Systems and processes	Climate	Outcomes for children
Colleagues know more about how children come to feel motivated to read.	Colleagues prioritise children's understanding of fluency over task completion.	There is an assessment system that provides colleagues with useful information about children's reading attainment but with minimal workload.	Colleagues feel that they belong to a staff team that is good at teaching reading.	Children participate fully in reading lessons.
Colleagues know more about how to run a calm and purposeful classroom.	Colleagues are better at directing the attention of the least advantaged children towards reading.	There is a quality assurance system that provides leaders with useful information about the strengths/areas for improvement in the teaching of reading fluency without negatively affecting climate.		Children feel successful and enjoy reading.

Colleagues' knowledge	Colleagues' behaviour	Systems and processes	Climate	Outcomes for children
	Colleagues use strategies to run calm and purposeful reading lessons.	There is a system for intervening when children fall behind in reading fluency to help them keep up.		Children feel that they belong to a peer group who identify as readers.
	Colleagues engage in reading CPD.	There is a termly review of the reading curriculum and sequences of learning.		
	Colleagues use reading lesson time effectively.	There is a termly review of the content of reading interventions and pedagogy.		

Example 2: Improving maths attainment in lower Key Stage 2 for children not yet fluent in recall of number facts/calculations

Colleagues' knowledge	Colleagues' behaviour	Systems and processes	Climate	Outcomes for children
Colleagues know more about how children gain automaticity of number facts/fluency of calculation.	Colleagues have higher expectations of all in terms of their effort and what they are capable of in maths lessons, particularly those disadvantaged in some way (paying attention, quality feedback).	Leaders provide regular and iterative CPD opportunities for colleagues to get better at teaching maths, including collaborative planning.	Colleagues feel that they have autonomy over how they teach maths.	Children achieve well in statutory tests (multiplication tables check/Key Stage 2 SATs).

Colleagues' knowledge	Colleagues' behaviour	Systems and processes	Climate	Outcomes for children
Colleagues understand the chosen maths programme (including common misconceptions) and the school's maths strategy.	Colleagues explain mathematical concepts clearly, presenting new ideas in small steps and with scaffolding.	Leaders present a clear school strategy for the teaching of maths, including active ingredients understood by all.	Colleagues experience flow when planning and teaching maths (clear goals, just the right difficulty and deeply satisfying).	Children achieve well in internal assessments (automaticity of number facts/fluency of calculation).
Colleagues know more about the active ingredients of the maths strategy and how to teach automaticity of number facts/fluency of calculation.	Colleagues are better at responsive teaching – checking understanding and addressing misconceptions.	There is a coherent, well-sequenced maths curriculum that is well resourced.	Colleagues have a clear purpose for the teaching of maths.	Children with SEND support plans meet relevant short-term targets for maths.

Colleagues' knowledge	Colleagues' behaviour	Systems and processes	Climate	Outcomes for children
Colleagues know more about how children come to feel motivated in maths.	Colleagues prioritise mathematical understanding over task completion.	There is an assessment system that provides colleagues with useful information about what children know and what they do not but with minimal workload.	Colleagues feel that they belong to a staff team that is good at teaching maths.	Children participate fully in maths lessons.
Colleagues know more about how to run a calm and purposeful classroom.	Colleagues design mathematical tasks where scaffolds are gradually removed.	There is a quality assurance system that provides leaders with useful information about the strengths/areas for improvement in the teaching of mathematical fluency without negatively affecting climate.		Children feel successful and enjoy maths.

Colleagues' knowledge	Colleagues' behaviour	Systems and processes	Climate	Outcomes for children
	Colleagues are better at directing the attention of the least advantaged children towards mathematical concepts.	There is a system for intervening when children fall behind with mathematical fluency to help them keep up.		Children feel that they belong to a peer group who identify as mathematicians.
	Colleagues use strategies to run calm and purposeful maths lessons.	There is a termly review of the maths overview and sequencing in medium-term plans.		

Colleagues' knowledge	Colleagues' behaviour	Systems and processes	Climate	Outcomes for children
	Colleagues engage in maths CPD.	There is a termly review of the content of maths interventions and pedagogy.		
	Colleagues use maths lesson time effectively.			

Example 3: Improving behaviour during break and lunch in upper Key Stage 2

Colleagues' knowledge	Colleagues' behaviour	Systems and processes	Climate	Outcomes for children
Colleagues know more about how to set and maintain social norms for unstructured times in line with school policy.	Colleagues have higher expectations of the behaviour of all at break and lunch, particularly those disadvantaged in some way.	Rules around behaviour at break and lunch are consistently reinforced.	Colleagues feel that they have autonomy over how they manage behaviour.	Children follow adult direction and self-regulate.
Colleagues know more about the active ingredients of the behaviour strategy.	Colleagues elevate visibility of desirable break and lunch social norms.	There is equality of adult authority in the eyes of the children.	Colleagues experience flow when managing behaviour (clear goals, just the right difficulty and deeply satisfying).	Children treat each other respectfully and kindness is the default.

Colleagues' knowledge	Colleagues' behaviour	Systems and processes	Climate	Outcomes for children
Colleagues know more about how children come to feel motivated.	Colleagues amplify approval of desirable break and lunch social norms.	Leaders provide regular and iterative CPD opportunities for adults to get better at managing behaviour at break and lunch.	Colleagues have a clear purpose – a shared vision for behaviour at break and lunch.	Children participate enthusiastically in activities at break and lunch.
Colleagues know more about the parts of the school where behaviour can be more challenging and why.	Colleagues signal children's status to show that they belong when talking about break and lunch (and beyond).	There is a behaviour system that recognises children's successes and that triggers escalated responses for persistent undesirable behaviours.	Colleagues feel that they belong to a staff team that is good at managing behaviour.	Children feel successful and enjoy school.

Colleagues' knowledge	Colleagues' behaviour	Systems and processes	Climate	Outcomes for children
Colleagues know more about the kind of break and lunchtime activities where behaviour can be more challenging and why.	Colleagues cultivate affinity to show that children belong.	Social, emotional and mental health (SEMH) screening occurs twice yearly.	Colleagues feel supported by leaders when dealing with challenging behaviour.	Children feel that they belong to a peer group, class and school community.
Colleagues know more about how individual children react best to different strategies.	Colleagues earn trust through consistency and care in interactions at break and lunch.	Purposeful games are run at break and lunch and there are a variety of activities set out each day for children to engage in.		Children trust adults.

Colleagues' knowledge	Colleagues' behaviour	Systems and processes	Climate	Outcomes for children
Colleagues recognise their own biases when it comes to children's behaviour.	Colleagues engage in behaviour CPD.			Children feel safe at school.
	Kindness is the default for colleagues.			
	Colleagues deal with negative break/lunch behaviour swiftly and fairly.			

Example 4: Improving provision for children with SEND/who are disadvantaged in writing

Colleagues' knowledge	Colleagues' behaviour	Systems and processes	Climate	Outcomes for children
Colleagues know more about how children learn to write (both transcription and composition).	Colleagues have higher expectations of all in terms of effort and what they are capable of in writing lessons, particularly those disadvantaged in some way (paying attention, quality feedback).	Leaders provide regular and iterative CPD opportunities for colleagues to get better at teaching writing, with high expectations and appropriate scaffolding.	Colleagues feel that they have autonomy over how they teach writing/support children with SEND.	The least advantaged children achieve well in statutory tests (ELGs/SATs).

Colleagues' knowledge	Colleagues' behaviour	Systems and processes	Climate	Outcomes for children
Colleagues understand the specific barriers to learning to write associated with having different special educational needs or being disadvantaged in other ways.	Colleagues explain concepts such as sentence construction clearly, presenting new ideas in small steps and scaffolding.	Leaders present a clear school strategy for writing, SEND provision and tackling disadvantage, including active ingredients understood by all.	Colleagues experience flow when planning and teaching writing/ supporting children with SEND (clear goals, just the right difficulty and deeply satisfying), with the least advantaged in mind.	The least advantaged children achieve well in internal assessments of writing.
Colleagues know more about the active ingredients of the school's strategies for teaching writing, SEND provision and tackling disadvantage.	Colleagues are better at responsive teaching – checking understanding and addressing misconceptions.	There is a coherent, well-sequenced writing curriculum that is well resourced.	Colleagues have a clear purpose for supporting SEND and teaching writing.	Children with SEND support plans meet their short-term targets on writing, catching up to the point where they no longer need a plan (where appropriate).

Colleagues' knowledge	Colleagues' behaviour	Systems and processes	Climate	Outcomes for children
Colleagues know more about how children come to feel motivated.	Colleagues prioritise understanding sentence construction over task completion.	There is an assessment system that provides colleagues with useful information about children's understanding of sentence construction but with minimal workload.	Colleagues feel that they belong to a staff team that is good at teaching writing and supporting children with SEND.	The least advantaged children participate fully in writing lessons.
Colleagues know more about how to run a calm and purposeful classroom.	Colleagues are better at directing the attention of the least advantaged children towards holding a sentence in their heads and rehearsing it.	There is a quality assurance system that provides leaders with useful information about the strengths/areas for improvement in the teaching of writing/SEND support, without negatively affecting climate.		The least advantaged children feel successful at writing and enjoy school.

Colleagues' knowledge	Colleagues' behaviour	Systems and processes	Climate	Outcomes for children
Colleagues know more about the SEND code of practice and the implications on writing of common special educational needs.	Colleagues use strategies to run calm and purposeful lessons.	There is a system for intervening when children fall behind in sentence-level work to help them keep up.		The least advantaged children feel that they belong to a peer group/the class/the school community.
Colleagues know more about the individual children with SEND/who are disadvantaged, including their unique barriers to learning to write and what is needed to overcome them.	Colleagues engage in writing and SEND CPD.	There is a termly cycle of assess, plan, do, review for children on the SEND register (which is updated regularly).		The least advantaged children can write accurate sentences fluently and enjoy writing.

Example 5: Improving the coherence and the sequencing of the history curriculum

Colleagues' knowledge	Colleagues' behaviour	Systems and processes	Climate	Outcomes for children
Colleagues know more about how children learn historical knowledge and concepts.	Colleagues have higher expectations of all in history lessons, particularly those disadvantaged in some way (paying attention, quality feedback).	Leaders provide regular and iterative CPD opportunities for colleagues to build history subject knowledge and to get better at teaching history.	Colleagues feel that they have autonomy over how they teach history (and, to a certain extent, curriculum content choices).	Children achieve well in internal assessments (composite tasks at the end of each unit of work, quizzes).

Colleagues' knowledge	Colleagues' behaviour	Systems and processes	Climate	Outcomes for children
Colleagues know more about how children come to feel motivated.	Colleagues explain historical knowledge and concepts clearly, presenting new ideas in small steps and scaffolding.	There is a coherent, well-sequenced history curriculum that is the progress model – conceptual development across years and key stages and clarity over the discipline of history.	Colleagues experience flow when planning and teaching history (clear goals, just the right difficulty and deeply satisfying).	Children participate fully in history lessons.

Colleagues' knowledge	Colleagues' behaviour	Systems and processes	Climate	Outcomes for children
Colleagues have a better historical subject knowledge of the units of work that they teach and their place in the curriculum as a whole.	Colleagues are better at responsive teaching – checking understanding and addressing misconceptions.	There is a quality assurance system that provides leaders with useful information about the strengths/areas for improvement in the history curriculum, without negatively affecting climate.	Colleagues have a clear purpose for the teaching of history.	Children feel successful and enjoy history.

Colleagues' knowledge	Colleagues' behaviour	Systems and processes	Climate	Outcomes for children
Colleagues have a better understanding of the historical and substantive concepts that thread through the curriculum and how each unit of work builds on previous ones.	Colleagues prioritise historical understanding over task completion.	There is a termly review of the history overview and medium-term plans to refine coherence and content choice.	Colleagues feel that they belong to a staff team that is good at teaching history.	The least advantaged children feel that they belong to a peer group/the class/the school community.
Colleagues know more about the discipline of historical inquiry.	Colleagues are better at directing the attention of the least advantaged children towards historical concepts.			

Colleagues' knowledge	Colleagues' behaviour	Systems and processes	Climate	Outcomes for children
	Colleagues use strategies to run calm and purposeful history lessons.			
	Colleagues engage in history CPD.			
	Colleagues clearly explain the discipline of history – what historians do and the ways of knowing.			

References

Bereiter, C. and Scardamalia, M. (1993), *Surpassing Ourselves: An Inquiry Into the Nature and Implications of Expertise*. Chicago: Open Court.

Bryk, A. and Schneider, B. (2003), *Trust in Schools: A Core Resource for Improvement*. New York: Russell Sage Foundation.

Clear, J. (2018), *Atomic Habits: An Easy & Proven Way to Build Good Habits and Break Bad Ones*. London: Penguin Random House.

Coe, R. (2014), 'Classroom observation: It's harder than you think', Centre for Evaluation & Monitoring, www.cem.org/blog/414

Coe, R., Aloisi, C., Higgins, S. and Major, L. E. (2014), 'What makes great teaching? Review of the underpinning research', Sutton Trust, www.suttontrust.com/wp-content/uploads/2014/10/What-Makes-Great-Teaching-REPORT.pdf

Coe, R., Rauch, C. J., Kime, S. and Singleton, D. (2020), 'Great teaching toolkit: Evidence review', Evidenced Based Education, www.cambridgeinternational.org/Images/584543-great-teaching-toolkit-evidence-review.pdf

Cordingley, P., Higgins, S., Greany, T., Buckler, N., Coles-Jordan, D., Crisp, B., Saunders, L. and Coe, R. (2015), 'Developing great teaching: Lessons from the international reviews into effective professional development', Teacher Development Trust, https://dro.dur.ac.uk/15834/1/15834.pdf?DDD45+DDD29+DDO128+hsmz78+d700tmt

Evans, M. (2020), 'Surviving and thriving in uncertainty', in S. Lock (ed), *The ResearchED Guide to Leadership: An Evidence-Informed Guide for Teachers*. Woodbridge: John Catt Educational.

Fletcher-Wood, H. (2018), *Responsive Teaching: Cognitive Science and Formative Assessment in Practice*. New York: Routledge.

Kirschner, P. A., Sweller, J. and Clark, R. E. (2006), 'Why minimal guidance during instruction does not work: An analysis of the failure of constructivist, discovery, problem-based, experiential, and inquiry-based teaching', *Educational Psychologist*, 41, (2), 75–86.

Kraft, M. A. and Papay, J. P. (2014), 'Can professional environments in schools promote teacher development? Explaining heterogeneity in returns to teaching experience', *Educational Effectiveness and Policy Analysis*, 36, (4), 476–500.

Leithwood, K., Harris, A. and Hopkins, D. (2019), 'Seven strong claims about successful school leadership revisited', *School Leadership & Management*, 40, (1), 5–22.

Leithwood, K., Sun, J. and Pollock, K. (eds) (2017), *How School Leaders Contribute to Student Success: The Four Paths Framework.* New York: Springer.

Mccrea, P. (2017), *Memorable Teaching: Leveraging Memory to Build Deep and Durable Learning in the Classroom.* CreateSpace Independent Publishing Platform.

Mccrea, P. (2020), *Motivated Teaching: Harnessing the Science of Motivation to Boost Attention and Effort in the Classroom.* CreateSpace Independent Publishing Platform.

Mowles, C. (2021) *Complexity: A Key Idea for Business and Society.* New York: Routledge.

Pink, D. H. (2009), *Drive: The Surprising Truth About What Motivates Us.* Edinburgh: Canongate.

Robinson, V. (2011), *Student Centred Leadership.* San Francisco: Jossey-Bass.

Robinson, V. (2017), 'Capabilities required for leading improvement: Challenges for researchers and developers', https://research.acer.edu.au/cgi/viewcontent.cgi?article=1306&context=research_conference

Rosenthal, R. and Jacobson, L. (1968), 'Pygmalion in the classroom', *The Urban Review*, 3, 16–20.

Schein, E. H. (1985), *Organizational Culture and Leadership.* San Francisco: Jossey-Bass.

Walker, M., Worth, J. and Van den Brande, J. (2019), 'Teacher workload survey 2019: Research report', NfER, https://assets.publishing.service.gov.uk/government/uploads/system/uploads/attachment_data/file/855933/teacher_workload_survey_2019_main_report_amended.pdf

Wiliam, D. (2006), 'Assessment for learning: Why, what and how', https://view.officeapps.live.com/op/view.aspx?src=https%3A%2F%2Fwww.dylanwiliam.org%2FDylan_Wiliams_website%2FPapers_files%2FCambridge%2520AfL%2520keynote.doc

Wiliam, D. (2010), 'Teacher quality: Why it matters, and how to get more of it', https://dylanwiliam.org/Dylan_Wiliams_website/Papers_files/Spectator%20talk.doc

Wiliam, D. (2012), 'Every teacher can improve', https://www.youtube.com/watch?v=eqRcpA5rYTE&feature=emb_title

Worth, J. and Van den Brande, J. (2020), 'Teacher autonomy: How does it relate to job satisfaction and retention?', NFER, www.nfer.ac.uk/media/3874/teacher_autonomy_how_does_it_relate_to_job_satisfaction_and_retention.pdf

Index

Page numbers in *italics* and **bold** denote figures and tables, respectively.